The Conflict

By
Wilson Awasu

Airleaf Publishing

airleaf.com

ISBN: 1-60002-035-6

Library of Congress Cat Card: 2006924951

Contents

Part 5: Resistance

Part 6: Rationale

Introduction

Imagine. Jesus went to Bethlehem on his 31st. birthday. Peter, Andrew, James, John and the others were with him. In his usual style he pitched an open-air pulpit at a corner in the open-air market. "Repent for the kingdom of God is at hand," he said in a loud clear voice. Again he said, "Repent for the day of the Lord's favor is here."

A voice shrilled from the crowd, "Who are you?"

"I am Jesus, Son of David. My other name is Immanuel[1]. I am the child and son Isaiah said will be called 'Wonderful, Counselor, Mighty God, Everlasting Father, and Prince of Peace…'"[2].

"Shut up," an angry alto voice butted in. "Peace, what do you know about peace? You were the child Herod wanted to kill. Our sons died. You lived. Talk about peace? Rachel is still weeping for her dead children"[3].

Another voice bellowed, "Yes, yes, it's him. Stone him, stone him." A mob rushed on Jesus to lynch him. Peter and his colleagues, trying to fence them off were like straw in wild fire. Somehow Jesus wriggled out of sight, singed.

The apostles later caught up with Jesus on the northern exit of Bethlehem. They asked "What was all that about?" Apparently they hadn't heard about Jesus' childhood flight to Egypt. So he told them[4]. Insightfully, James said, "The people are angry because

God saved you but didn't save their sons from Herod's sword."

But why didn't God? Shortly after that visit, Herod II cut off John the Baptizer's head. That was Jesus' herald. Why didn't God stop Herod II? James who had made the observation above later lost his head to the sword of Herod III. Why didn't God stop this Herod and the other two? He could.

Consider the Herods. Were they right in killing infants Jesus' age, Jesus' herald, and Jesus' apostle? Why did they do it? Did they act alone? Who else was involved? What was at stake? Was Satan connected with it? Did the Herods know he was?

How about Peter, did he know it? A moment earlier God had used him to declare that Jesus was the Messiah. A moment later, Satan too used Peter's vocal apparatus to counsel Jesus not to die like the Messiah. Jesus' rebuke, "Get out, Satan" showed that Jesus saw Satan at work in Peter[5]. Why didn't Peter see it?

Another time, Jesus must have known that Judas, another one of his disciples, had agreed to sell him to the Pharisees. But Jesus didn't confront Judas about it, or order him to go do it. But as soon as Satan entered Judas, Jesus ordered, "Go do quickly what you're about to do"[6].

This doesn't sound right, Judas, one of the 12, selling Jesus to the Pharisees; the Pharisees, the strictest party of God's servants buying Jesus for 30 pieces of silver to kill him? Why? How long did Satan stay in Judas when he entered him? Did Satan enter the

Pharisees also, all of them at the same time? How could he?

What linked the Herods, Judas, Satan and the Pharisees (and Pilate) together? If it was God-defiance and hatred for Jesus, then certainly, Satan's must have preceded the Herods', Judas' and the Pharisees'. Satan knew about the birth of Jesus at the time Eve and Adam fell in the Garden of Eden. That was when God promised that Jesus would be born to defeat Satan[7]. Therefore Satan must have hated Jesus from then.

Satan's own God-defiance preceded that. Recall. God-defiance, born and carried out by Lucifer was what turned Lucifer into Satan[8]. But why did people's God-defiance and hatred for Jesus become the uniting force and ferry to the death of Jesus[9]?

The churches at Ephesus, Pergamum, Thyatira, Sardis and Laodicea[10] didn't hate Jesus like the Pharisees and Judas and the Herods and Satan. But didn't they defy God by trading Jesus for orthodoxy and legalism, false teachers and false teaching, and hypocrisy and worldliness? Why did they? Who was the buyer? That was only 60 years after Jesus' resurrection, ascension and enthronement[11]. How could it be?

That's a puzzle. So is this. Jesus prayed all his life on earth. After his enthronement over all rule and authority, power and dominion, he and the Spirit now pray for the saints. Why? The martyred saints asked God to avenge them on their lynchers. But God said "No, not yet." Not yet, how much longer?[12].

The reality lingers and insists. Satan's and people's God-defiance and hatred for God intertwine fighting God and God's purpose. Where do we look for answers? Speculation plays into the hand of Satan, the father of lies[13]. **The Conflict** is a biblical exegetical study I did to address the never ending conflict between God and Satan, raging between "yes" to satanic principles of defiance, force, greed, selfishness and evil ambition, and "yes" to God, God's word and God's Spirit.

The Study highlights

- habitual and biblical reality of the conflict
- myths about the conflict
- forms of the conflict
- battlegrounds of the conflict
- resistance and overcome in the conflict, and
- rationale for the conflict, and rationale for resistance and overcome in the conflict.

The Conflict invites us to biblically know that we aren't like Bethlehem, Peter, Judas, the Herods, and the five churches fighting God and God's purpose unawares in an on-going conflict between God and Satan. Rather, we're deliberate and God-dependent in fighting with God in the conflict.

Part 1: Reality

Chapter 1
Habitual

Do Christians have one God but serve many gods? What do personal and corporate self-absorption say about that? Might the reality reveal on whose side we're fighting in the conflict between God and Satan?

Personal self-possession

Dave was an Accountant. He worked with a bank for bankers. He rose fast on the corporate ladder to become Vice President-Operations. The company knew him as hardworking and Christian.

Two years after he became VP, Dave, Pam and the family relocated to an elite part of town. Pam became a housewife when their babies began to arrive. She dropped out of the church choir, teaching Sunday school and prison ministries. Meanwhile Dave rose to the position of "Number 2" person in the bank. He served as chairman for a local chapter of the Boys Scouts, a local Parent-Teacher Association, and missions committee at church. His wife and kids saw him less and less. His usual excuse was busy-ness.

Then he and his personal secretary, Lillian grew close. Before long, an extra marital affair buzzed around them. Pam picked up the gossip first at a doctor's office. Later, a former colleague called offering a listening ear. At church that Sunday, Pam overheard people talking about it. She went investigating.

Lipstick brush-offs on collars of a number of Dave's shirts shocked her. Double stubs of movie, theater and opera tickets she pulled out of Dave's pockets alarmed her. It drove her mad to discover inconsistencies in Dave's business travel schedules. A peek in Dave's cell phone voicemail box choked her.

Pam confronted Dave. He denied everything. He accused Pam of distrust. He charged, "You're just like everyone else. You all envy me of my success."

"No I'm not," Pam said.

"Yes you are. You believe everyone but your husband," Dave said.

"Listen to you, Dave. When will you face facts?"

"When you stop accusing me falsely," Dave said.

"Enough, I'm out of here," Pam said.

"Fine with me," Dave said.

Pam and Dave separated. In two weeks Pam died. Two weeks after Pam's funeral, Dave asked Lillian to marry him. Before she declined, she asked, "Will I keep my job if I say no?"

Dave thought for a moment. In a flash he realized that expedience had ruled everything he'd done. That included the marriage proposal to Lillian. What alarmed him was that he didn't feel sorry at the realization. He framed charges and fired Lillian. It took Nellie, who replaced Lillian to jolt Dave's conscience.

Nellie refused to be bullied into compliance. In a heated debate between Dave and Nellie in Dave's office, Nellie jabbed him, "How many lives will it take to get you off your high horse?"

"And what is my high horse?" Dave demanded.

"Egoism" Nellie thundered and stalked out of Dave's office, slamming the door behind her.

Dave sunk in silence. At first he felt humiliated. But soon, humiliation hatched conviction and repentance. Dave admitted to himself, for the first time, he was egoistic. He wept. He prayed. He asked for forgiveness and freedom from vestiges of self-possession. He felt peace melting down his body. Joy swelled in his heart and pressed his lungs against his ribs and out written all over his body.

Many things remained undo-able. Pay back was possible in a few. Dave retraced his steps and realized that selfish ambition had become his passion. He did whatever his will dictated. In the process, his opinions, preferences and views assumed finality. Personal advantage took over. What he did and what it did for him were all that mattered. In that way, Dave subjugated God's will, word, ways and works to his.

Thus self-absorption had become Dave's number one goal—his real god—in life. But self-worship, like all gods, demands expensive sacrifices[1]. Dave's included his relationship with family and Jesus. Any wonder that institutions share in this behavior?

Corporate self-possession

An evangelical seminary used three committees to fire a senior student just before his wife divorced him. Dick was his name. Why? How? Committee #1 acted on charges Dick's wife, Betty, leveled against him, and separated them. Dick stayed in a singles' dorm off campus. His visits to their on-campus apartment were limited, pre-arranged, approved and policed by Committee #1.

At 2:00 am one morning, Cliff, a colleague in the dorm challenged Dick to take responsibility for his part in husband and wife quarrels. Dick called Betty right then and apologized. "Come on home," Betty said.

Three weeks later Dick returned to the dorm. Committee #2 had agreed with Betty it was premature for them to get back together. In a conversation, Dick thanked Cliff for his counsel and encouragement. But he lamented, "Betty resents counseling with a student. So we can't see you as a couple."

"Had any of our professors volunteered to help save your marriage?" Cliff asked.

"No," Dick said.

"Not even our professors in counseling?"

Dick said "No," shaking his head.

Dick had three units left to graduate in the Master of Divinity program. Divorce was now not only imminent. It was inevitable. The seminary set up Committee #3 to establish a basis to fire Dick. Cliff was one of the students who appeared before the committee.

Addressing the chairman he said, "Mr. Chairman, in my conversations with Dick, I learned that since the troubles between Dick and Betty reached seminary authorities, Dick was only made to appear before committees. None of our faculty volunteered counseling Dick and Betty personally as fellow believers should[2]. That tells me on occasion spiritual leaders could divorce their lifestyle from what they preach. That contradicts what you've taught us. The anomaly prevents me from saying anything against Dick, even if I had something to say."

But based on the advice of Committee #3, the seminary fired Dick the next day. His charge was "gross misconduct." Everyone knew the real reason. The seminary would lose financial support for graduating a divorcee. To prevent that, the seminary failed to be merciful and understanding—godly. It substituted its will, word, ways and works for God's without realizing it. It served another god—institutional self-absorption—while teaching belief in one God.

Two weeks to graduation in another evangelical seminary, the Academic Affairs Committee agreed to graduate Bobby, a doctoral candidate, with a masters degree. His supervisor, professor Duke, had declared Bobby's dissertation sub-standard.

The student-rep on the committee, Wes, disagreed and said so. He argued that Bobby had already made professor Duke the talk of campus. Many students agreed with Bobby that professor Duke was callous. He should have known and told Bobby the state of his dissertation much earlier than two-plus weeks to graduation. He had been supervising Bobby's project for four years.

The chairman of the committee asked Wes what he thought was best to do. "Reconcile Bobby and professor Duke to each other," Wes said.

"We must not mix academic affairs with pastoral affairs" professor Baron, a prominent member of faculty retorted. After a gnawing silence, the chairman asked Wes to recommend a line of action.

Wes volunteered to pastor and mentor Bobby as a fellow student. He challenged the committee, all faculty members, to find a way to pastor and mentor their colleague into reconciliation with his doctoral student. The committee took the challenge. Bobby graduated with a doctorate degree in two months.

Like the former, the latter seminary was trapped in institutional protocol turned god. But unlike the former, the latter admitted the folly. It allowed God's will, word, ways and works to tamper with its own as it should. But why do we individually and corporately pit our will, word, ways, and works against God's so often and don't see it or admit it? Look at these duels.

God's will vs. our will

At the time of writing, a missionary friend, Larry confided. A church that had supported him with 55% of his budget was about to withdraw its support. A theological tension had developed between him and this church. Contrary to a theological view he and they had shared, circumstances in ministry context had forced him to pray for the sick.

It delighted him that some of the sick were healed. But it saddened him that his delight failed to gladden his supporters. They threatened, "Stop praying for the sick or you'll lose our support." What should he do?

God's word vs. our word

Three soon-to-be national leaders helped missionary Chuck unpack and fix up his plastic Christmas tree. They helped him decorate it. He lighted it just before the others arrived for the day's discipleship lesson.

He taught Jesus' birth from Luke. His disciples wished to know the link between the Christmas tree and that account. How should he answer? On what basis would he suggest an equivalent for their use?

God's ways vs. our ways

Five years ago Barbara became the President of a mission agency. She discovered a decaying under-layer that contradicted the appearance of life on the surface. Nasty interpersonal clashes mocked team-work in the field. Defiant disagreements wedged the field and home offices. Attrition stalked the agency.

Among others, she pushed spiritual formation to remedy the organizational defects she inherited. She also made spiritual formation a major piece in the criteria for missionary recruitment. Strangely, numbers of new missionaries dropped by 80%. Financial support dropped by 65%.

Her Board of Trustees found that intolerable. They pushed her to mount an aggressive missionary recruitment campaign. That meant she watered down her emphasis on personal spirituality of missionary recruits. Her job and reputation stood on the line. How should she respond? What would be the basis of her response?

God's works vs. our works

Bob wept at a Sunday school class, confessing, "For 35 years I have transplanted my home church in missions. I had charged leaders I trained and appointed for lacking initiative, ownership, and vision. I resented their dependency and flogged them for it.

"Only recently did I realize we caused all that through transplanted churches. We carved people to fit the transplant. In hindsight, we would have avoided the mess if we had planted churches with converts to Jesus instead. As it is we've stunted people's faith and stifled their initiative. Worst of all, we stand between people and Jesus. How can God forgive such arrogance?" Bob dropped to his seat sobbing.

How would he be consoled, and on what basis?

These scenarios are only the tip of the iceberg. But they shout, one, the human will always defies God while deifying humanity[3]. Two, human words produce death when substituted for God's word which is life and spirit[4]. Three, human ways rob God of glory and holiness while obscuring them to people[5].

For God insists "My thoughts are not your thoughts, neither are your ways my ways, says the LORD. For as the heavens are higher than the earth, so are my ways higher than your ways and my thoughts than your thoughts"[6]. Four, human works—acts of salvation—always replace "God-grace-faith" with "human-works-merits."

That means conflicts generate when self-absorption leads the way. But self-absorption is self-worship. And self-worship is the worship of another god. Self-god attracts or gravitates to other gods in alliance and allegiance fighting God and us. What becomes of our professed worship of one God? How do we interpret and deal with the resulting contradiction and conflict? The biblical reality of the conflict sheds light on the reality.

Chapter 2
Biblical

Jesus grew up in Nazareth. He and the Nazareth synagogue knew each other. But in adulthood that synagogue turned on him to kill him. Why? Jesus read his job description from Isaiah 61:1-2 to the synagogue in Nazareth.

> The Spirit of the Lord is upon me, because he has anointed me to preach good news to the poor. He has sent me to proclaim release to the captives and recovery of sight to the blind, to set at liberty those who are oppressed, to proclaim the acceptable year of the Lord[1].

"Ridiculous. When did the carpenter turn the teacher? Stop him before he brings the wrath of God on Nazareth for tolerating a false prophet"[2], the synagogue said. They jostled Jesus to the edge of a cliff to push him over. However, Jesus slipped through their hands and left the crowd[3].

What turned his hometown synagogue against him? What made the synagogue sure they knew God's will for Jesus? God would thank them for killing him, why? No answers, but so began the death chase for Jesus. His bitterest pursuers were the Pharisees, people who knew the Scriptures inside out.

Early one morning Jesus taught in the temple[4]. The Pharisees opposed him. Jesus dismissed their opposition with Scripture[5]. Answering a query, he said, "Truly, truly, I say to you, before Abraham was, I am."

"Shut up. You're not yet 50 and you're older than Abraham?" some said.

"Stone him," others said. They took stones and rushed on him. But Jesus hid himself and went out of the temple[6].

Another time, Jesus admitted in the temple that he was the Son of God. He added that he and the Father are one.

"Blasphemy," the Pharisees screamed. They rushed on him to tear him to pieces. Again, Jesus slipped out of their claws. He was gone, safe[7].

Jesus taught in the temple again. Ordinary people heard him gladly. Unimpressed, the Pharisees mobbed him. They demanded a copy of his vita. He told them stories illustrating God's mercy for merciless managers. The Pharisees saw themselves in the stories. Outraged, they neared him like tigers, red-eyed, snarling death.

But nonverbally, the audience expressed disgust and dismay at elite theologians turned thugs. Jesus' current popularity rang. They heard it and quit. Regrouping, they planned stealthier ways to trap Jesus and destroy him[8].

Theologian bureaucrats went at it first. They cornered Jesus with a sly argument for and against Jews paying taxes to Rome. A yes or no answer would mean disloyalty to Abraham or Caesar. Give it, and Jesus would give them cause to arrest him and turn him over to the civil authorities. Jesus outwitted them, "Give to Caesar what belongs to Caesar. And give to God what belongs to God." They failed to trap him[9].

Then Satan entered Judas, one of the twelve, and he betrayed Jesus to the Pharisees[10]. Did they see Satan in Judas? Where was Satan when they mock-tried Jesus, handed him over to Pilate and pressed for the death sentence? Did they see themselves as collaborators with Satan, Judas, Pilate and Rome to kill Jesus?[11].

They were sure they served God while rejecting Jesus and killing him. But Pilate saw envy in their hypocrisy[12]. Envy pitted their will, word, ways and works against God's. But they didn't see it. That didn't excuse it.

Herod I too envied the baby Jesus. He barely missed killing him. He killed the Bethlehemite infants instead[13]. Did Herod's envy collaborate with Satan as did the Pharisees'? How about Haman about 400 years before Jesus was born?

All Haman knew was that he hated Mordecai and his people. He obtained an imperial decree to annihilate all Jews. Had the decree not backfired through the fasting and prayer of Queen Esther, Mordecai and others, Haman would have wiped out the ancestral line of Jesus. Haman's ignorance of the fact was a non-issue. Was Satan exploiting Haman's hatred unseen?

Personal responsibility aside, what role did Satan play in the cumulative effects of Israel's idolatry, namely,

- Aaron and Jeroboam's golden calves[14]
- Manasseh's institutionalized idolatry[15]

that led to the Assyrian and Babylonian conquests and exiles[16], preceding the Persian (Haman)?

The pattern is clear. Pitting human will, word, ways and works against God's always results in disaster. Why? As said earlier, the act either attracts or gravitates to Satan. The effects fight God's purpose, defying God. That explains Babel[17], the people of Noah's day[18], Cain and Lamech[19], and Eve and Adam[20].

Though it backfired, resulting in many nations and many languages, Babel had formed to sever humanity from its Creator. Before Babel, human God-defiance had exploded. God punished it with a deluge. Only Noah and his family survived. Earlier, Lamech bragged about rampant murders. Before him, Cain walked past God's warning and killed his brother Abel.

This is a proneness Eve and Adam bequeathed humanity in their God-defiance. Properly interpreted, Eve and Adam's God-defiance was

- no to God, and yes to Satan
- loss of freedom and life in God, and enslavement and death under Satan
- loss of God-likeness, namely righteousness and holiness and love, and Satan-likeness, namely, defiance, force, greed, selfishness and evil ambition
- loss of rule over creation under God, and bondage to the tyranny of Satan.

That spelt total loss for God if he left it at that. Satan won. But it was right here that God put enmity, conflict, between Satan and Jesus. Jesus would suffer in the process of redeeming lost and dead humanity. Satan would lose fighting and lose self-defeated.

Satan set out to prove God wrong. He must prevent Jesus from being born. Failing that, kill him to abort the match. Satan always hides in human God-defiance to conceal his presence and acts. People ally with him to their peril. They help his cause against God and themselves. They become willing victims in the process.

This conflict raged since Lucifer became Satan, and Eve and Adam lost paradise. Incidentally even Jesus' death, resurrection and enthronement over all rule and authority, power and dominion haven't ended it. That Jesus and the Holy Spirit pray for the saints on top of that, complicates matters. Do myths resolve matters? Could they?

Part 2: Myths

Chapter 3
Myth 1: No Conflict

There's no conflict, says myth 1. Why? Jesus' death and resurrection ended the conflict between God and Satan, and between Satan's kingdom and God's kingdom. Good idea. But it contradicts at least three outcomes of the victory of Jesus. They are

- the celebration of the enthronement of Jesus[1]
- the demonstration of the wisdom of God[2]
- the coronation of the enthroned Jesus[3].

Each of those outcomes says the conflict continues.

One, the celebration of the enthronement of Jesus

Ephesians 1:18-22 says,

> I pray…that you may know…that power… which he [God] exerted in Christ when he raised him from the dead and seated him at his right hand in the heavenly realms, far above all rule and authority, power and dominion, and every title that can be given, not only in the present age but also in the one to come. And God has placed all things under his feet…

The "all," "every," and "all" in the above passage say no power or title in this world or the next is exempt from the sovereignty of Jesus. The dominion that God had intended humans to have—but lost through Eve and Adam's rebellion[4]—is now exercised by Jesus alone.

Jesus said so himself, "Fear not, I am the first and the last, and the living one; I died, and behold I am alive forevermore, and I have the keys of Death and Hades,"[5]. Earlier he had said, all authority in heaven and on earth is now his. In term's of it, he sent his disciples into the world to make disciples of all peoples[6]. The same reality makes Jesus the judge of all things[7].

There it is. An all-wise God would only enthrone the resurrected and ascended Jesus over forces that exist and pose a threat. Why? Though defeated, God-defiant forces haven't conceded defeat. Outraged they fight back, venting their hatred for God on believers in Jesus.

In view of that[8] Jesus had warned that his followers would be persecuted just like the prophets who preceded him predicting his coming. From experience Paul added "All who desire to live a godly life in Christ Jesus will be persecuted"[9].

Abel[10], Stephen[11] and other martyrs[12] asked God "How long before you judge and avenge [us on those who killed us]?" God's response, "They were each given a white robe and told to rest a little longer, until the number of their fellow servants and their brethren should be complete, who were to be killed as they themselves had been"[13].

Martyrs from before and after Jesus, how many more to be martyred? How much longer? All that says the conflict goes on for followers of Jesus who dare to celebrate Jesus' enthronement. Compromisers might escape the raw deal of the conflict. But they live with unavoidable contradiction, staleness, a form of the reality of the conflict. Why?

Having a spiritual life in a fleshly body to live in a world ruled by satanic principles of defiance, force, greed, selfishness and evil ambition can't help being in conflict. In addition, Ephesians 6:10-20 and 2 Corinthians 10:3-5 talk about a battle gear. Believers are to wear it as a lifestyle. Why would God give believers a battle gear for a non-existent battle?[14].

Two, the demonstration of the wisdom of God

Another outcome of the victory of Jesus is that "now, through the Church, the manifold wisdom of God should be made known to the rulers and authorities in the heavenly realms"[15]. 1 Corinthians 2:8 adds, if those rulers and authorities—Satan, and the invisible power of sin and death, plus their contemporary human allies, the Sanhedrin, Pilate and Rome,—understood that wisdom, they wouldn't have killed Jesus.

What was that wisdom? Why must the now Church, not the future Church, show it? And why show the wisdom of God to "the rulers and authorities in the heavenly realms"? Apparently it's not enough for Jesus to be enthroned in the heavenly realms over those powers. Rather, by dint of the reality, the still defiant forces must see and feel their defeat.

One way they see and feel their defeat is losing victims to Jesus[16]. People they had held in bondage to the grip and ravages of

- satanic principles of defiance, force, greed, selfishness and evil ambition[17]
- divisions and hate, fear and distrust, hostility and violence[18]

are freed and transformed and empowered.

The freed feel so free they defy societal, political, religious, personal etc God-defiance. They wouldn't give it the last word in their lives any longer. Unafraid they give the last word in their lives on right and wrong, good and bad, and true and false to God, God's word, and God's Spirit instead.

Specifically, the freed love, forgive, and reconcile with one another across social, cultural, racial, ethnic, etc lines[19]. Unity in diversity dances in joy, peace and harmony where fear, divisions and hate had been. How can defeated forces refusing to concede defeat help being outraged? Why wouldn't they fight back, seeking to end the "madness"? But could they?

Three, the coronation of the enthroned Jesus

Jesus' birth, public ministry, death, resurrection, ascension and enthronement anticipate his coronation. At his coronation lost paradise returns, and humanity returns to the tree of life. Death, mourning, crying, pain and the old order of things disappear. God makes all things new[20]. Then Jesus unites with his Bride, the Church. He is crowned King of kings and Lord of lords.

Jesus' coronation consummates salvation in Jesus. The Scriptures[21] say Satan would form a people-spirits coalition to resist the consummation. This is business as usual for Satan. Using a similar coalition, "the rulers of this age"[22], he had resisted the provision of salvation in Jesus. It's unlike Satan to quiet down doing nothing in-between the provision and consummation of salvation in Jesus.

Rather, outraged, Satan would fight even harder to frustrate the transmission of the benefits of Jesus' death, resurrection and enthronement. Typically, he would hide behind the God-defiance of people and spirits, exploiting it. Tragically if we aren't consciously fighting on Jesus' side in the conflict we're unconsciously, and willfully sometimes, fighting on Satan's side; Jesus insists[23].

Chapter 4
Myth 2: Satan

Satan is the conflict, myth 2 says. In one sense of the myth, we are helpless against Satan. In another sense, Satan bothers people who bother him.

The helpless view

The helpless view cites Judas Iscariot[1] and Ananias and Sapphira[2] as typical. Satan filled the former to betray Jesus, and the latter to lie to and abuse the Holy Spirit. Meaning, Judas and Ananias and Sapphira were helpless against Satan's invasions. So are we all, myth 2 insists.

The myth ignores this. Though said to be filled by Satan, Ananias and Sapphira died for lying to the Spirit and abusing him. Concerning Judas' betrayal, Jesus had said, "The Son of man goes as it is written of him, but woe to that man by whom the Son of man is betrayed! It would have been better for that man if he had not been born"[3]. Why would a just God punish people for actions of Satan?

The "bother-not" view

This view warns, anyone who dabbles in the occult, or with mediums, magic, in short with the esoteric, like

King Saul[4] asks for trouble with Satan. Don't bother him and he won't you.

The Scriptures disagree. King Saul got into trouble through God-defiance. He rejected God's word and decided to do his own word[5]. The evil spirit that came to torment Saul on and off consequently, came from God, not Satan[6].

But even Judas and Ananias and Sapphira were minding their own business, not bothering Satan, when he filled them. How about Peter? A moment earlier God spoke through him, declaring Jesus as the Christ, the Son of God[7]. A moment later Satan used Peter's vocal apparatus, counseling Jesus to admit he was the Christ but refuse to die like him[8]. Peter wasn't bothering Satan. Neither were Eve and Adam when they entangled humanity (us) in Satan-likeness[9].

As for Job it was God who put him on the line and invited Satan to the fight. Satan went to afflict Job with intense suffering and loss from the presence of God (the book of Job). Job wasn't at all bothering Satan to be bothered by him.

However, pushed to logical conclusion, the helpless view of myth 2 teaches us to fear Satan. The bother-not view teaches us to disregard Satan. Both views are flawed twice. One, Satan is one of the entities outraged against us (see chapters 17-22). And according to Jesus the outraged remain indivisible[10].

Two, blaming Satan for our conflict makes him more powerful than God. He makes Holy Spirit-filled people unholy and unloving, prayerless and merciless, for example. Tragic, deception always plays into the hand of the father of lies, Satan[11].

Chapter 5
Myth 3: Demons

Unlike myth 2, myth 3 says demons are the conflict. Part of the myth sees demons in everything that goes wrong in our lives. The other part insists demonization is always demon possession. Demons possess things, places and people. And always these possessions are identifiable by any believer. Consistently, view one teaches active response; view two teaches passive, laidback, response.

The active response

Active responses look like this. Curse and exorcise demons when your cookies burn while you are busy doing many house chores all at once. Curse and exorcise demons when your car battery dies at 30 degrees below zero on a winter day in a parking lot after work. Curse demons when you lock your car keys in your car while the engine runs.

Curse demons when the police give you a speeding ticket. Curse demons when your temper and appetite control you. Whenever you can't have your way, demons are resisting you. Curse them. Curse and exorcise demons out of every delinquent child. The list is endless.

Extreme views see demons behind all sicknesses. Therefore the view forbids medical treatment for sicknesses including the medically curable. The reason, medical science can't diagnose demonic acts.

The solution, exorcise. Find a Scripture verse and pray alone or with other like-minded believers for deliverance. Holders base the view on Jesus' public ministry. He often exorcised demons[1]. He gave authority to the apostles and the 72 to do the same when he sent them on short-term mission trips[2].

Unfortunately, the basis of support for the view is its undoing. True, Jesus affirmed the 72 for effective exorcism. But he cautioned them to rejoice more in having their names written in heaven. They were saved and sealed by the Holy Spirit into Jesus[3].

Continuing, Jesus disclosed that he had seen Satan fall like lightning from heaven. But because he had given them authority to overcome all, note the word "all," the power of Satan, nothing of his would harm them. Jesus distinguished between Satan and demons. Adding, Satan's activities include demonic activity but go beyond them.

The laidback response

But like the active, the laidback response to demons is also flawed. Believers don't always readily identify the presence and activity of demons. Take Paul for example. It took several days before he identified a spirit of divination is a medium at Philippi[4].

Then there were the 7 sons of high priest Sceva[5]. Laidback, they presumed to exorcise a demon. The demoniac said, "Jesus I know and Paul I know, but who are you?" He beat them. And they ran out wounded and naked for dear life[6].

The active isn't that haphazard. It

- discerns berserk spiritual hierarchies and habitats[7]
- develops warfare principles and formulas[8]
- runs warfare ministries[9]
- reports spiritual warfare breakthroughs[10].

But active or laidback, scapegoating or stereotyping demons sees our conflict "out there." It fragments the -outraged fighting us "in-here" (see chapters 17-22). Jesus insists on indivisible kingdom of the outraged ruled by Satan[11]. Making demons the conflict overlooks the worst enemy in the conflict, which is, us.

Our unwillingness to give our "yes" to God, God's word, and God's Spirit—the last word—on good and bad, right and wrong, true and false gets us more in trouble than demons and Satan could. Why? That proneness is a repackage of satanic principles of defiance, force, greed, selfishness and evil ambition. In the final analysis, the proneness makes us defy God to Satan's delight. Why? Satan doesn't have to pull the strings to have what he wants. It's presented to him on a platter.

Chapter 6
Myth 4: The Occult

Myth 4 makes the practice of witchcraft, satanism and spiritism (all of which I call "the occult" in this book) the conflict. Occult practitioners play the most part, the myth insists. They place spells and curses on people; invoke demons and assign them to affect situations, people and homes.

Family feuds, church splits, and civil wars; inter-tribal and inter-racial tensions; and political party rivalries; parental and juvenile delinquency; injustice, oppression, exploitation and violence, etc. are all the work of the occult. In short, the occult is a plague. The vaccine for protection against this plague is, hate practitioners, boycott their business and merchandise, stay away from their homes, resorts and chain of hotels, and avoid talking about the occult.

It's true the Scriptures warn against occult practice.

> Let no one be found among you who sacrifices his son or daughter in the fire, who practices divination or sorcery, interprets omens, engages in witchcraft, or casts spells, or who is a medium or spiritist or who consults the dead. Anyone who does these things is detestable to the Lord[1].

In addition, the experience of Philip in Samaria[2], Barnabas and Paul in Paphos[3], and Paul in Ephesus[4] show that the occult could hinder evangelism and discipleship. Not only that, churches could be wrecked by occult practitioners cloaked in pastors, theologians and professors[5].

Then there is the influence of the occult that reaches our family rooms via the media. Glamorized, media products like horror movies, witches, magic, etc, trivialize the mystery of the occult. They make it look harmless and entertaining, to be accepted as a normal part of day to day living[6].

But there again, scapegoating the occult fragments a conflict in which the outraged hardly work alone (see chapters 17-22). In addition, myth 4 too overlooks our worst enemy, our post-conversion God-defiance. Only supposed Spirit-filled (we) can lie to the Spirit, abuse him, resist him, grieve him or quench him. What happens when we do? Having one God, do we serve many, and one of them is us?

Four myths about the conflict aren't all. But they illustrate the point. Myths may be popular. But they're dangerous. They trivialize a deadly conflict, trying to tie up issues God has left at loose ends[7].

For example, try all we can, we may never know

- why God allowed Satan to live after he'd rebelled against him, taking down a third of angelic population with him

- why God sent archangel Michael to help an angel fight an evil spirit-hold-off instead of crushing it
- why Jesus granted the request of legion demons to live after he'd exorcized them.
- why Jesus called Satan the ruler of this world
- why Jesus conquered Satan through his death and resurrection but didn't destroy him

And we may never know why God didn't stop

- Herod I from slaughtering infants in Bethlehem?
- Herod II from murdering John the Baptizer?
- Herod III from beheading James?
- the Sanhedrin from lynching Stephen?

Aside of all that, why do Jesus and the Holy Spirit pray for the saints when Jesus is enthroned over all rule and authority, power and dominion? Why haven't the enthronement of Jesus and the prayers of Jesus and the Holy Spirit stopped the saints (us) from self-love, self-seeking to self-serve?

Unbiblical, or partially biblical, interpretations of that kind of dilemma blind us to the conflict. We take the wrong side in it unawares. We're prepped to miss our God-given solution in it. Provoked in the conflict, we either acquiesce to what's provoking us or reciprocate it. Either way, we lose. We dishonor God.

Truly biblical views, on the other hand, unmask the reality and denial of the conflict. They strip forms and battlegrounds of the conflict. They focus our God-given resistance and overcome in the conflict. And they give us rationale to the conflict and resistance in it. Why settle for less?

Part 3: Forms

Chapter 7
Demonic

When the conflict is purely spiritual, agents are demons, evil angels and Satan. But who are they? And what do they do? How does who they are and what they do affect us? Where do we turn for clues?

Recall Job's disasters[8]. What would the media and meteorology have told us about Job's disasters, losses and sufferings? Wouldn't their microphones and lenses and radar have failed to detect Satan behind the Sabean and Chaldean raids, the brush fires and the tornadoes that took away Job's livestock, servants and children in one day[9]? But with graphic snapshots, backed by experts' validations we would be convinced the media and meteorology gave us the truth about Job's disasters.

Remember King Saul. What if psychiatry, clinical psychology and theology were our sole informants to educate us about his depression and fear? Would we know that there was an evil spirit involved? Would we be hinted that the evil spirit came to torment Saul after the Spirit of God had left him? Which of those informants could show that the evil spirit came at God's command[10]? How much did we really know if we claimed that we knew Saul's condition from those sources?

Another, what if medical science were all we had to educate us on the woman bent into two with her face a foot and half from her knees looking backward. Would we know that Satan was the cause?[11]. Would surgery and body reconstruction have normalized a body that Satan had crippled and wanted to trap crippled? Truth sometimes looks more fiction than fiction. Doesn't it?

Recall the prophet Micaiah. He stood alone among the prophets of his day when he refused to play the political game and enjoy King Ahab's favors[12]. But for Micaiah, nobody would have known that an evil spirit came at God's command to cause regular prophets to lie to the king. Micaiah suffered for telling the king the truth while his colleagues lied to him and went scot-free. But contrary to their lies, the king died in battle just as Micaiah had predicted.

The Holy Spirit predicted an increase of the work of lying spirits in the last days[13]. Their work would turn many believers away from Jesus Christ. They will follow lying spirits and false teaching instead. The success of those lying spirits lies in the credibility of the prophets and theologians that they seduce.

Seduced to do what? Tell the lie as truth and truth as the lie. And have the many believe it. That explains why, for example, many Christians don't believe in the existence of demons; and why myths, stereotypes and scapegoats, eclipse biblical truth and existential truth about the conflict.

It's unbiblical to see a demon in everything. For then we would demonize everything. It is also unbiblical to exclude demons in everything. When we do, we would humanize everything. Equally, it is unbiblical to stereotype demonization. For then we restrict them to the stereotypical, possessions and formulas for handling them[7].

So preoccupied, we miss demonic activities lying beyond the reach of media-meteorological, psychiatric-psychological, and medical-theological validations. So then, demonizations in daily life that could be interpreted medically or spiritually or psychologically or all three together pose a complex problem.

For from biblical perspectives, we know that demons afflict people with dumbness[8], blindness[9], epileptic seizures[10], insanity[11] and suicidal mania[12]. How do you tell the chemically, biologically, etc induced from the spiritual? When are self-inflicted injuries[13], supernatural strength[14], and physical deformation and dysfunction[15] natural or unnatural therefore demonic?.

It is not enough to know that Matthew 10:1, 12:43, Mark 1:23-24, Luke 4:33, 36 call demons unclean, impure, evil and foul spirits. It is also not enough to know that demons are vicious and malicious[16]; that there are degrees of wickedness in their ranks[17]; and that when demons gain control over a human body, they can come and go at will[18]. Or once by default, we exorcise a demon[19].

A bigger problem is this. We need to be biblically knowledgeable and biblically effective in unleashing God's message of freedom and life to any and all human situations, the demonic inclusive. And as usual, Jesus is our model.

Mark 5:1-20 talks about a demonic situation where several thousands of demons filled a respectable man and reduced him to a shameless beast of a man abandoned to live and die in cemeteries. When they met Jesus, they asked him not to send them out of their geographic area.

And Jesus granted their request. He ordered them out of the man and let them enter a herd of pigs grazing nearby. The pigs numbering 2,000 stampeded and drowned in a lake. Jesus must have known that the pigs would die but the spirits would live. Why did he let them?

Obsession with freeing the victim would rid me of biblical considerations for demons. Not so Jesus, why? Jesus and they, the demons and Satan for that matter, know two things I need to remind myself about often. One, Jesus is their destroyer because he is their conqueror[20]. Two, Jesus would destroy them on the judgment day not before. That was why demons protested whenever they met him "Have you come to destroy us before the time?"[21].

Meaning, accurate discernment and effective handling of demonic presence and activity would always credit absolute authority to Jesus Christ to advance the kingdom of God[22]. On the contrary, inaccurate discerning and haphazard handling of demonic situations would not only backfire[23]. It would retain seeking demonized people and occult victims in bondage through false assurance.

We return to this. We will miss it if our will, word, ways and works half-shaped by a mechanistic-secularistic mindset and behavior; and half-shaped by theological-denominational mindset and behavior, lead the way. On the other hand, a mindset and behavior shaped and governed by God, God's word and God's Spirit will discern and deal with the subtlest demonic or satanic masquerades.

Chapter 8
Evil Angelic

Evil angels are different from demons. But like demons and all citizens of Satan's kingdom, they too are possessed and driven by satanic principles of defiance, force, greed, selfishness and evil ambition. Therefore they don't wait for cues from Satan all the time before they resist God's purpose.

But who are they and where do they live? What are some of the ways in which they resist God? How does their resistance to God affect us? How do we help them against God and us? The Old and New Testaments shed light.

In the Old Testament we hear of the "holy ones" forming a heavenly court over which the Lord himself presides[1]; and "sons of God" in Job, the Psalms and Genesis 6:3.

Further, Deuteronomy 32:8 says, "God fixed bounds of all peoples according to the number of the sons of God. For the Lord's portion is his people, Jacob his allotted heritage." Earlier, Deuteronomy 4:19 had said that God had assigned the moon, the stars, and the hosts of heaven to the peoples under heaven. To the people of Israel he appointed himself.

That seems to echo God making many nations at Babel[2]; choosing Abraham to make out of him a nation serving the one true God[3]. God set the boundaries of the nations. He also set their times[4]. His purpose "was that the nations should seek after him…though he is not far from any of us,"[5]. But the nations didn't.

Why did the nations worship and serve the moon, the stars, the hosts of heaven instead? Was it the moon, the stars, the hosts of heaven that forced the nations to worship and serve them? Or was it the nations that worshipped "the creature" instead of the Creator?[6]. And did the worshipped "creature" become a god by accepting worship that is due only to God, the Creator?

In a sense it doesn't matter which preceded the other. For, usurped worship and undue worship make the object of worship a god. Whatever is worshipped does indeed become a god[7]. From God's perspectives, the worshipped is guilty for either usurping worship or accepting worship. And the worshippers are guilty for giving it.

But if the creature in Romans 1:25 equals the moon-the stars-the hosts of heaven in Deuteronomy 4:19 equals the sons of God in Deuteronomy 32:8, then the sons of God here, like all angelic beings, should know better. They should know that they and people and all creation are meant to worship and serve God and him only[8].

Why did they usurp or accept worship? Had they rebelled against God prior to this time? Or they hadn't. But they just exercised their will against God like all creatures are free to do? Would what the New Testament say about evil angels help?

New Testament writers describe evil forces as follows: principalities, powers, rulers, dominions, thrones, names, princes, lords, gods, angels, spirits, unclean spirits, wicked spirits, and elemental spirits.

Often, the descriptions lend themselves to varied interpretations. For example, "When they bring you before the synagogues and the rulers and authorities"[9] talks about people. So does Acts 4:26 when it says, "The kings of the earth set themselves in array and the rulers were gathered together against the Lord and his Anointed."

On the other hand, the powers and thrones and authorities in Colossians 1:16, 2:15; Romans 8:38; Ephesians 6:12 are superhuman. But the rulers, the authorities and governing authorities in 1 Corinthians 2:8, Titus 3:1 and Romans 13:1 imply the combination of both people and superhuman powers.

Mostly, however, the New Testament uses these terms to describe superhuman agencies in the spiritual realms[10]. Jesus[11] speaks of the devil and his angels. Revelation 16:13 makes them lieutenants of Satan[12]. Paul saw them as demonic agencies in league with Satan[13].

Put together, "the creature"[14], "the hosts of heaven"[15], "the sons of God"[16] or the angelic princes of nations[17] became gods either by accepting worship or usurping it. Having become gods, through ceasing to be conduits of worship to God, they were prepped to collaborate with Satan to deceive their respective people.

They see angels from God as intruders in their territory. They censor them. The angelic prince over Persia must be typical. That prince, Daniel 10 tells us, withheld for 21 days an angel God had sent to Daniel. Only through archangel Michael's help was he freed to go and deliver God's message to Daniel.

Therefore evil angels must include the one-third angelic population Satan whipped out of heaven, and angelic guardians God had assigned to the nations that had turned God-defiant[18]. As celestial beings they are powerful because God hasn't taken from them the power he gave them. They are wicked because their rebellion against God converted their God-given desire to choose to love God into hatred for God and his purpose. And they are subtle because they can take our unbiblical views about them and use them to their advantage.

For example our disbelief in their existence frees them to do as they please and we take responsibility for their abuse of us. We humanize the demonic. On the other hand an obsessive belief in them makes us fear them. We hold them responsible for everything that goes wrong while exonerating ourselves of all human responsibility. We demonize the human. Either way, we delight them, not Jesus.

I agree with Michael Green. He sees "the air" and "the heavenly places" in Ephesians 2:2 and 6:12 as the surroundings of the material world, not the home of God. Evil angels live there. They interpenetrate the climate of countries; "the trends of their politics and nuances of their cultures"[19].

John Stott[20] adds. That makes us and our social, political, judicial, and economic, etc., structures vulnerable indeed[21]. How? The latter don't see it, know it or admit it when their insistence on being the final word on life attracts or gravitates to evil angelic God-defiance. Only through letting God, God's word and God's Spirit have the last word sheds needed light. Only that light energizes the saints (us) to swim against the current, when swamped with institutionalized God-defiance.

Chapter 9
Direct Satanic

The Satan who doesn't exist until there's need to scapegoat him must be fictional. But when invoked he's present everywhere. He becomes more powerful than God. He takes Spirit-filled Christians hostage, making them lie to the Spirit; abuse him, resist him, grieve him and quench him. Here's a case in point.

A missionary team

On a 5-couple missionary team, four couples were friends from college. A medical doctor, a registered nurse, an agriculturist, an economist, two linguists, two engineers, and two theologians, plus eight kids between 1-12 years formed the team. The adults and kids had a two-day in-house orientation to their agency and a preview of their project.

In addition adults and kids had a five-week out-source pre-field cross-cultural training in skills for learning a new language; understanding home-culture, field-culture and personal values; discerning and handling interpersonal conflicts; and managing personal spirituality. Finally, adults and kids had on-field orientation to the field and an overview of their particular project.

Then language and culture learning began. Each family had a chain of intercessors and supporters, family and friends back home praying for them. The home and field offices prayed for them weekly. The field director visited the team monthly. What could possibly go wrong?

After six months, a couple returned home. Reason, culture shock wiped wife out. Second language acquisition stressed out several members on the team. Interpersonal conflicts built and stalked proving irresolvable.

The second year ending, two husbands returned home for a 3-month clinical psychological treatment and rejoined their colleagues. Six years passed and interpersonal conflicts remained ugly and defiant. Close to the end of the 7th year, the team admitted it wasn't working. The team split and returned home, leaving members embittered and blame-shifting; feeling defeated, disappointed and disillusioned. The team and the agency concluded that Satan routed the team.

Which Satan was that, the fictional or the real one? Fictional or real, that Satan must be more powerful than God. He routed 10 Spirit-filled foot soldiers of Jesus, mocking the prayers of the home and field offices and supporters. Did Satan continue to exist in the aftermath? How would the agency and team show that he did? How biblical or unbiblical were the team and agency's views and treatment of Satan?

Who is Satan?

The Bible says Satan is the devil, the old serpent, the dragon, the deceiver and ruler of the world system[1]. He is the god of this world[2]. The whole world lies in his control[3].

Other synonyms of Satan include Beelzebub and Beliar; the strong one and the wicked one; the accuser and the tempter; the adversary and the enemy; the liar and the murderer; the prince of this world and the prince of the power of the air. "The air" that immediately surrounds the material world became Satan's habitation after God had driven him from heaven. Co-inhabitants are the third angelic population that joined Satan to rebel against God[4].

Satan has intelligence. It far exceeds that of people because God created him a celestial being[5]. He designs schemes beyond human understanding. He lures and entraps people[6].

Satan also has a mind, knowledge and memory. He quoted Psalm 91:11-12 out of memory to Jesus when he tempted him[7]. In addition, Satan has a will, pride, wrath and organizational abilities. He speaks. He spoke to Eve in the garden. And he spoke to God when he appeared before God uninvited[8]. He also spoke to Jesus when he tempted him in the desert[9].

Satan performs miracles[10]. He does not always come as a roaring lion[11]. Often he masquerades as an angel of light[12]. Satan marshals everything he is and has against God's purpose in direct and indirect ways.

Examples of the direct

Satan seduced Eve and Adam into rebellion against God[13]. Satan attacked Job to get him to deny God[14].

Satan wrestled with the archangel Michael over Moses' corpse[15]. In a vision, Zechariah saw Satan accusing Jesus personified as Joshua before God[16].

Just before Jesus started his public ministry, Satan met him face-to-face. He tempted him, as he had done Eve and Adam, to defect from God[17]. Satan used Peter's vocal apparatus to tell Jesus the same thing. He pressed Jesus to admit he was the Christ but refuse to die as the Christ[18]. Luke 22, Satan entered Judas Iscariot before he betrayed Jesus to the Sanhedrin. Between the betrayal and the arrest of Jesus, Satan asked Jesus to let him have the apostles and sift them like wheat[19].

At a future date, Satan will incarnate in the antichrist. The antichrist, Satan's superman will be a powerful world ruler. Satan will empower him with superhuman intellect, power and hatred for God and his people. His reign will be a blend of demonic and human activity[20].

Paul discerned that it was Satan who stopped him from going to see the Thessalonian believers[21]. He differentiated between this hindrance and the Holy Spirit's redirection in Asia minor[22]. Then in Acts 5:1-11, Peter disclosed that Satan filled Ananias and Sapphira when they lied to and abused the Holy Spirit.

This particular incident parallels two prior ones. The other two involved Nadab and Abihu[23], and Achan[24]. The three incidents occurred at significant new beginnings. Nadab-Abihu stood at the inauguration of the Levitical priesthood. Achan did at the brink of entering the promised land. Ananias-Sapphira stood at the dawn of the Church age.

The three incidents were self-grafting deceptions in those new beginnings. Unexposed and un-eliminated at once, they would integrate in those beginnings. Each of the incidents ended in sudden death. God struck Nadab and Abihu dead instantly. At Joshua's command Israel stoned and burned Achan, his family and animals. Ananias and Sapphira dropped dead at Peter's word.

The incidents are similar and dissimilar. Satan filled Ananias and Sapphira, not Nadab and Abihu and Achan. Yet all three incidents aimed at wrecking new beginnings of God before they set. But God held Nadab, Abihu, Achan, Ananias and Sapphira responsible for their actions whether they were under Satan's influence or not.

On what basis did a just God do that? Why? What are the implications? Those concerns bring us to Satan's indirect activities.

Chapter 10
Indirect Satanic

To Satan's advantage, God-defiant people and spirits are formed by satanic principles of defiance, force, greed, selfishness and evil ambition. Like Satan, they all hate "the light."

> And this is the judgment, that the light has come into the world, and men loved darkness rather than the light, because their deeds are evil. For everyone who does evil hates the light, and does not come to the light, lest his deeds should be exposed. But he who does what is true comes to the light, that it may be clearly seen that his deeds have been done in God[1].

That means Satan has minions who like him see Jesus Christ as the light of God that exposes evil. Therefore, all on their own, God-defiant people and spirits fight the light whenever and wherever it discomforts them. Their evil nature and ability to fight the light becomes vehicle for the satanic. Evil actions that responsible people and spirits must take responsibility for, become Satan's indirect way of getting at God.

Examples of the indirect

Thus Eve and Adam's rebellion[2]; Cain's murder of Abel, and Lamech's rampant murders[3]; explosion of evil that led to the deluge in Noah's day[4]; and Babel's revolt[5], were indirect satanic sabotages shot at God and his purpose. What for? It was to prevent Jesus, conqueror of Satan, from being born[6]. Satan didn't engineer those activities. But they served his purpose.

Genesis 12, God narrowed down the coming of Jesus, Satan's conqueror, to Abraham. Satan followed. In usual fashion, satanic principles of defiance, force, greed, selfishness and evil ambition in people provided vehicle. Through genocide and an imperial decree respectively, Pharaoh[7] and Haman[8] attempted and failed to annihilate Abraham's descendants.

Herod I didn't know he served Satan's purpose when he tried to kill the baby Jesus[9]. But had he succeeded he would have stopped Jesus from ever meeting Satan to defeat him. Satan confirmed the fact when he met Jesus face-to-face thirty years later[10]. He pressed but failed to get Jesus to defect from God. He went back to working concealed.

Like Herod, Haman, and Pharaoh, the Pharisees didn't know they enlisted in Satan's service through their hatred for Jesus. They hunted Jesus to the death. Their hunt met Satan at the end of the trail. But they didn't see him standing in Judas, who betrayed Jesus to them[11]. The collaboration allied Pilate. He went against all reason and judicial propriety and sentenced Jesus to death by crucifixion[12].

Pilate, like Pharaoh, Haman, Herod, and the Pharisees, wasn't possessed by Satan. But like them Pilate too was possessed by satanic principles of defiance, force, greed, selfishness, and evil ambition. As always, it is those principles that unite people to Satan against God and his purpose. That delights Satan who according to the Scriptures is "the dragon [that is] angry…and [goes] to make war…on those who keep the commandments of God and bear testimony to Jesus…"[13].

All the better for Satan, the Pharisees' hatred for Jesus outlived Jesus' crucifixion. It continued to be vehicle for Satan's indirect attacks on God. The Pharisees bribed the guards to bury the fact of the bodily resurrection of Jesus Christ. They imprisoned and flogged the apostles; stoned Stephen to death; and drove Jesus' followers out of Jerusalem[14].

Then Herod III too murdered James, the brother of John just like Herod II and Herod I had done John the Baptizer and the Bethlehemite infants respectfully. Rome tortured to death Jesus' followers to entertain the Caesars and their fans. Again Satan didn't engineer any of those acts. But each of them served him.

As said earlier, all it takes to become vehicle for Satan's indirect attack on God's purpose is to unleash

- pre-conversion God-defiance, namely, defiance, force, greed, selfishness and evil ambition, or
- its post-conversion repackage, namely, unwillingness to let God, God's word or

God's Spirit have the last word on good and bad, right and wrong, and true and false[15].

People in leadership or influential positions like teachers and parents, the media and entertainers etc., exercising authority, mind-control or influence over others are most strategic vehicles for Satan's indirect attack on God and his purpose. Their positions give them power, influence and sphere to misuse for greater damage and to Satan's delight.

So the Scriptures urge us to pray for all people particularly our political, social, religious, institutional leaders and all others who are in authority. Then we would live in peace and quietness, in godliness and dignity[16].

Even so, Jesus says Satan's kingdom of God-defiance remains indivisible. Its magnetic field, (satanic principles of defiance, force, greed, selfishness and evil ambition), is everywhere sucking in likeminded, human or spiritual. Did it suck in the missionary team and agency in the story above? How? Are governments free from the magnetic field, particularly when they flirt with satanic principles of defiance, force, greed, selfishness and evil ambition?

Chapter 11
Intended Political

Governments are God's servants. But they serve Satan. True or false? If they do, how does that happen? Sequentially or simultaneously? Romans 13 and Revelation 13 give some answers.

First, Romans 13:1-7 says,

> Let every person be subject to governing authorities. For there is no authority except from God, and those that exist have been instituted by God. Therefore [one] who resists authority resists what God has appointed, and those who resist will incur judgment.
>
> For rulers are not a terror to good conduct, but to bad. Would you have no fear of [one] in authority? Then do what is good, and you will have praise from the same: for he is a servant of God to you for good. But if you do that which is evil, be afraid; for he does not bear the sword in vain: for he is the servant of God, an avenger for wrath to him that does evil.
>
> Therefore you must be in subjection, not only because of the wrath, but also for the sake of conscience. For this cause you pay taxes, for they are servants of God's service, attending

continually upon this very thing. Give to all their dues; taxes to whom taxes are due; revenue to whom revenue; respect to whom respect; and honor to whom honor.

In contrast, Revelation 13:1-18 says,

And the dragon stood on the shore of the sea. And I saw a beast coming out of the sea. He had ten horns and seven heads, and with ten crowns on his horns, and on each head a blasphemous name. The beast I saw resembled a leopard, but had feet like those of a bear and a mouth like that of a lion. The dragon gave the beast his power and his throne and great authority. One of the heads of the beast seemed to have had a fatal wound, but the fatal wound had been healed. The whole world was astonished and followed the beast. Men worshipped the dragon because he had given authority to the beast, and they also worshipped the beast and asked "Who is like the beast? Who can make war against him?"

The beast was given a mouth to utter proud words and blasphemies and to exercise his authority for forty-two months. He opened his mouth to blaspheme God, and to slander his name and his dwelling place and those who live in heaven. He was given power to make war against the saints and to conquer them. And he was given authority over every tribe and people and language and nation. All inhabitants of the earth will worship the beast—all whose names have not been written in the book of life belonging to the Lamb that was slain from the creation of the world

Then I saw another beast, coming out of the earth. He had two horns like a lamb, but he spoke like a dragon. He exercised all the authority of the first beast on his behalf, and the earth and its inhabitants worshipped the first beast...And he performed great and miraculous signs, even causing fire to come from heaven to earth in full view of men. Because of the signs he was given power to do on behalf of the first beast, he deceived the inhabitants of the earth. He ordered them to set up an image in honor of the [first] beast...He was given power to give breath to the image of the first beast, so that it could speak and cause all who refused to worship the image to be killed. He also forced everyone, small and great, rich and poor, free and slave, to receive a mark on his right hand or on his forehead, so that no one could buy or sell unless he had the mark, which is the name of the beast or the number of his name. This calls for wisdom. If anyone has insight, let him calculate the number of the beast, for it is a man's number. His number is 666.

Romans 13 vis-à-vis Revelation 13

The chart below sharp focuses the differences between the governing systems Romans 13 and Revelation 13 describe.

Romans 13	**Revelation 13**
Governing Authorities	**Governing Authorities**
Derive origin, dignity, right, sanction, power and authority from God	Derive origin, dignity, right, sanction, power and authority from Satan
Are servants of God	Are servants of Satan, blaspheming God's name, dwelling place and followers
Govern on God's behalf	Govern on Satan's behalf
Rule over respective nations	Rule over all nations
Maintain law and order	Disregard law and order
Establish justice for all	Deny justice to some
Punish evildoers, being conduits of God's wrath against evil and appreciation for good conduct	War against the saints, being conduits of Satan's wrath against the saints and contempt for good conduct
Conduits of worship to God	Objects and usurpers of worship due only to God.

Receive willing submission and veneration from the ruled	Extort submission and veneration from the ruled

The contrasts between the nature, form and functions of the two sets of governing systems are diametrically opposed to each other. Each set is internally consistent and functional, vying for legitimacy. But how can that be? Romans 13:1 insists that "Everyone must submit to governing authorities, for there is no authority except" the ones God establishes?[1].

Countering that, Revelation 13:2b says, "The dragon [Satan] gave to the [first] beast [a human world ruler] his power and his throne and great authority." Does God allow Satan to establish governing authorities? Or, he doesn't. But Satan usurps those God instituted and then corrupts them? Most unlikely, because the satanic likeness in the ruling figures in Revelation 13 looks natural with them. They must have had it from before ascending to power.

How about timing? Is all this an end time occurrence? Satan will follow a thousand years imprisonment with a parole devoted to forming a global satanic government, to wage war on God[2]. Then there is the issue of submission to all governing authorities. Are we to regard and relate to governing authorities Satan sets up as God's servants in spite of their blasphemies?[3].

Submission to satanic rule escapes organized persecution. But blind submission compromises commitment to God. Are both the divine and the satanic institutional rule restricted to the political dimension? Do they include the social and religious? 2 Thessalonians 2:3-4, 9-10 provides some answers.

> Do not let anyone deceive you in any way, for the day will not come until the rebellion occurs and the man of lawlessness is revealed, the man doomed to destruction. He will oppose and exalt himself over everything that is called God or is worshipped, so that he sets himself up in God's temple, proclaiming himself to be God.
>
> The coming of the lawless one will be in accordance with the work of Satan displayed in all kinds of misleading miracles, signs and wonders and in every sort of evil that deceives those who are perishing. They perish because they refused to love the truth and so be saved.

There it is. At a future time in history, Satan will incarnate in a person. 2 Thessalonians 2:3 calls this individual "the man of sin or lawlessness…the man doomed to destruction." He must be the one Revelation 13:1-2 calls "the [first] beast—symbolic of a future world ruler. Daniel 7:24b-25 sees him as the eleventh king in the fourth kingdom. In 1 John 2:8 he is the "antichrist." To this devil in human form, Satan will give "his power and his throne and great authority"[4].

His "coming will be in accordance with the work of Satan displayed in all kinds of misleading miracles, signs and wonders, and in every sort of evil that deceives those who are perishing"[5]. He will be an intellectual genius, having and exercising great authority, full of hatred for God and his followers. He will oppose God while seeking to be worshiped as God[6].

During his reign the dragon (Satan), the beast (the devil incarnate) and the false prophet (a human agent of the first beast) will unleash an unprecedented demonic invasion. This will result in unparalleled demonic worship and activity[7].

The invisible army of demons[8] will seduce the rulers of the nations. Form a worldwide military alliance. And wage war on God and his people[9]. This foreshadows a future one world government, with Satan more visible at the head. Demons will stand side by side people to rule the world.

So the government as Satan's servant isn't yet. That means since Babel[10] the government should be God's servant. History books, war libraries, war museums and war movies disagree. The government has been anything but God's servant. Why? What happened?

Chapter 12
Demonized Political

At Babel[1] humanity felt powerful and self-sufficient. It tried to sever itself from God its Creator. That was a unanimous demonstration of Eve and Adam's legacy, satanic principles of defiance, force, greed, selfishness and evil ambition. But instead of independent humanity, Babel became many peoples and many languages.

Acts 17:26-27 says

> And he [God] made from one [Adam] every nation of [people] to live on all the face of the earth, having determined allotted periods and the boundaries of their habitation, that they should seek God, in the hope that they might feel after him and find him.

Humanity dispersed in language groups, forming people states, nations. Any wonder that the government as God's servant eluded the nations? But the period for the government as Satan's servant hadn't come. Yet subtly or overtly, governments abuse power and dominate people. And often citizens support government decisions, good or bad. Why?

National Idolatries

For example, what propels a nation to go to war with another to conquer, divide, exile, maim, and subjugate it? One people brutalizes another. Empires vandalize many peoples. They create colonies they rule at pleasure. They amass wealth through dehumanizing the conquered and colonized. The strong and powerful make the weak and powerless serve them. They monopolize for the enjoyment of the few, limitless freedoms and rights they deny the many who serve them[2].

Not too distant past examples include European colonization of Africa[3]; African slave trade[4]; Nazi Germany and the holocaust[5]; and Apartheid South Africa[6]. The aftermath lingers, haunting the world's conscience. What happened to the government as God's servant? Invaded? By what?

What is responsible for national idolatries? What makes a nation see pride, dignity and essence in terms of political genius, technological advancement, economic power, military machinery, petroleum industry, and/or cultural sophistry, to idolize them? Why does citizenry follow seeing pride, identity and essence in terms of national idols? Citizens may deny being devotees. But like devotees, they support unjust wars to protect those idols any time[7].

On the other hand, what makes formerly oppressed nations perpetrate dehumanization imposed by former oppressive nations? Though politically independent they trade their languages for oppressors' languages.

They pledge dependency; and stifled cultural, political, economic, technological self-expression, without visible external forces pulling the strings.

Or, there are hidden external forces pulling the strings? What is the point? Why would an ousted oppressor delight in disguised meddling in the affairs of the formerly oppressed? National bleeding economies show that the meddling is choking search for nationhood. To what extent is international politics an accomplice to this?

Why is international goodwill unable to resist the activities of international evil-will; and at a time when the world has supposedly become a global village? Why do suspicion, treachery, and violence stalk us into cocooning behind sensitive alarm systems and doubly bolted windows and doors?

Why are we not free in our boasted freedoms? All this smells of the presence and work of the antichrist (see immediately above). But he is not here yet. How then do we explain these horrors? What has taken the government as God's servant hostage?

The Only Resistance

The Scriptures say human sinfulness aside, the "spirit" and "power" of the antichrist stand behind national idolatries. How? The spirit and power of the antichrist have long preceded him. Said another way, the shadow of that reality had long invaded humanity.

"And as you have heard that the antichrist is coming, even now many antichrists have come"[8].

Compare "The spirit of antichrist which you have heard is coming and even now is already in the world,"[9] and

> …now you know what [the Church] is holding him back, so that he may be revealed at the proper time. For the secret power of lawlessness is already at work, but the one [Holy Spirit] who now holds it back will continue to do so till he is taken out of the way[10].

This is where the tragedy occurred. God placed the Holy Spirit and the Church on earth[11] to restrain the effects of the spirit and power of the antichrist that have preceded his arrival. The Spirit of God restrains the spiritual reality of the antichrist in the spiritual realm. The Church is to resist his already visible reality in the realm of people. The two go hand-in-hand.

Part of the Church's resistance is prayer.

> I urge you, first of all, to pray for all people. As you make your requests, plead for God's mercy upon them, and give thanks. Pray this way for kings and all others who are in authority, so that we can live in peace and quietness, in godliness and dignity. This is good and pleases God our Savior[12].

The other part consists of Christ-like living. That is radical obedience to God, God's word and God's Spirit; love, forgiveness, and goodwill to all people; and evangelism and discipleship. Blended, the Spirit's resistance in the unseen world and the Church's resistance in the seen create the context in which the government can be a servant of God[13].

Rulers in every culture, race, tribe, and language will serve the people they rule. They hold power lightly, seeing God as ultimate. They recognize they derive their origin, dignity, right, sanction, power and authority from God. They recognize that they are servants of God and therefore govern on God's behalf. They rule over respective nations without meddling in the affairs of other nations.

They maintain law and order and establish justice for all. They preserve and reward the good while deterring evil by punishing evildoers to correct and restore criminals to civility. They serve as conduits of worship to God, not through legislation of the worship of God but by example. They receive, not extort, submission and veneration from the ruled.

The Scriptures didn't say that the Holy Spirit's work nullifies the Church's, citizens' and the government's flirtation with satanic principles of defiance, force, greed, selfishness and evil ambition. On the contrary, flirtation with those principles attracts or gravitates to forces it delights, namely God-defiant evil angels and demons and Satan (see above). The spirit and power of the antichrist and the antichrist belong among these. How can we deny playing into their hands? How can we escape the effects of causes we contribute to?

Chapter 13
The Societal

Societies make governments. Governments make societies. But governments and societies are made by people. People too aren't free from the molding of societies and governments. It's a cycle for better or worse. Where does it all start? What's the glue? Is flirtation with satanic principles of defiance, force, greed, selfishness and evil ambition part of that glue?

Why is the pain of ridicule, ostracism, and sometimes death, the price people pay to unglue? Why does fear of the pain of ridicule, ostracism or death prevent many people from ungluing when government becomes demonic? Why does loyalty to a corrupt government and unjust society eclipse loyalty to God, God's word and God's Spirit for Christians?

What happens to the good news? Does the Church at that point side with governmental and societal God-defiance to mock the Spirit's resistance of the antichrist's spiritual reality in the invisible realm? Might not the un-resisted visible reality engulf government and society and people including Christians?

A church in Florida had supported 80% of missionary Julie Baker's budget. The church had done prayer walks in cities of Bulgaria on her invitation. But in 2003, Julie severed ties with that church. Why? The church rejected her choice of marriage partner, a Bulgarian male pastor.

The outcomes of those prayer walks paralleled the spiritual warfare breakthroughs that George Otis[1]; Tom White[2]; C. Peter Wagner[3], etc reported. Meaning, the church had effectively used spiritual warfare principles and formulas[4].

That was a sign of an adept spiritual warfare ministry[5]. The ministry sized up and toppled the Bulgarian bit of berserk spiritual hierarchies and habitats[6]. What tripped Julie's church?

It knew how to deal with an "out-there" conflict. But it lacked awareness about an "in-here" habitual conflict. The "in-here" conflict often hides in the socio-political dabbling in satanic principles of defiance, force, greed, selfishness and evil ambition. Our uncritical participation in the quagmire keeps us on the side of the world's divisions, hate and violence; biases and prejudices, and stereotypes and scapegoats.

But the quagmire begins to melt in a commitment to letting God, God's word and God's Spirit scrutinize our entire socialization after we become Christian. A sense of freedom and empowerment follow. Where to start? Take a peek at the socialization process.

Socialization

Social rules, regulations, traditions, customs, and ideas, views and beliefs about ourselves, others, God and gods, animals, nature and creation, in short, about reality don't exist outside of us. They are not even distinct of us. They are us. What we are, they are. What they are, we are. They and we are mutual products of each other.

From our earliest beginning, in our homes, schools, and churches or religions, popular culture (through the influence of media products and messages) begins to shape us in its likeness. It teaches us how to think, feel and act, and how not to think, feel and act.

We do not outgrow cultural ways as we do baby-clothes, childhood, adolescence, and youth. Rather, being shaped in the likeness of cultural ways, grows with us just like our mind and perception, bones, muscles and body, grasp of vocabulary and speech, and so on, do. That is the natural way of socialization.

Naturally, we grow up eating beef not goat, and potatoes not plantains. We wear baseball caps and not turbans. We learn to accept people that look like us and reject people that differ from us. We sacrifice events for time or time for events; activity for personal relationships or vice versa.

Similarly, we are appalled by ancestral veneration. But we see nothing wrong with rationalism. We resent sacrificing individual rights for the good of the group. But competitive, acquisitive, divisive, individualistic behaviors even when they violate the rights of the group, appeal to us. And while respect for and submission to authority appears stifling, questioning and rejecting authority in favor of individual rights feels normal and proper.

Those are examples of cultural behaviors. They are consistent with cultural values that spawn them. Some are me-first or self-sufficiency is the rule of life. Independence, mobility and freedom are deserved personal rights. Time is money. Youth is priceless, it is to be coveted.

Contrasting somewhat with those are, I am because we are. Relationships are priceless. Youth are immature therefore their opinion is to be rejected. Older people are wiser. Their opinion always carries.

The lists go on. But what makes cultural values so binding on us is a non-negotiable rightness that stands behind them validating them. The rightness consists of cultural ideas, views, beliefs or basic assumptions about reality. Here are some common ones.

Life is the outcome of material processes acting by chance. People are autonomous; therefore they are free to do as they please. All people are created equal. But some people are created inferior to others. People are biological machines; life ends at death. There's no ultimate foundation for ethics. Authority is arbitrary therefore it is evil. Satan is a myth. If you don't bother Satan, he wouldn't bother you. God ceased to work miracles, therefore be skeptical about the miraculous.

Others are, people are spiritual beings, human life is sacred, and nature too is sacred. Authority is God-given therefore it is good. People are interdependent and ultimately answerable to God. God created the universe but he is powerless against evil, therefore look for power, any power, in readiness to fight evil, etc.

We adopt these and similar "rightness" views about things—reality—unconsciously through socialization. Therefore, our views, values and ways of thinking, feeling and acting toward time, events, people, morality, good and bad, right and wrong, and true and false, and so on, are all part of us.

Socialization Scrutiny

Becoming a believer in Christ doesn't all of a sudden erase the cumulative effects of our socialization process. In fact, even our views, acceptance and practice of the way of Christ are consistent with our socialization, schooling and training.

No doubt, there is good in cultures and societies humans create. But there is also evil. For example, individuals may want God, but often they are caught in the web of family ties, religious structures and social systems that prevent them from doing so on pain of ridicule, persecution, ostracism or death[7].

It was from such perspectives that Gentile conversions failed to gladden Jewish believers in Jesus. Of more importance to them were their cultural norms. Peter violated them. They criticized him, "You went into the house of uncircumcised men and ate with them"[8]. To avoid being scolded a second time, Peter refrained from dining with non-Jews at Antioch as soon as culturally-correct ambassadors arrived from James[9]. Didn't Julie's church trip here similarly?

Earlier, in the Old Testament, it was right at home, between husband and wife, that culturally-correct Sarah ill-advised Abraham to have Ishmael with Hagar, her maid. That was an acceptable social practice of the time. But when Sarah and Abraham used that cultural form, they disobeyed God. This is how.

Isaac was to be born on the basis of "God-promise-grace-faith"[10]. His birth paralleled the birth of Jesus Christ our Lord and our birth into the kingdom of God. Sarah-Abraham scheme, tried to switch that basis to "human-works-merits" instead[11]. God stepped in and let Sarah and Abraham have Isaac in spite of themselves. But for centuries, including our own, the Ishmael-Isaac controversy remains unresolved.

Between personal sinful ways and society's sinful ways—our margin of freedom to think, feel, and act godly hinges on commitment to God, God's word and God's Spirit. Followed by an on-going discipline to let God, God's word and God's Spirit scrutinize all of our socialization, schooling and training to make us truly biblical in our cultural views and ideas, values and behaviors.

When we do, we will begin to see biases and prejudices built into exclusive rights, privileges and advantages; safety, security and comfort; we enjoy socio-culturally. The challenge comes. How far can we go addressing the biases and prejudices? Have others tried and failed to bring about change? How much of those rights, privileges and advantages are we willing to give up for Christ's sake? Are we willing to face the pain of ridicule, persecution, ostracism, or death for taking a stand socio-culturally?

What happens when we do nothing to be truly biblical? We Christianize societal (and/or) governmental God-defiance by condoning it. The basis of our silence is fear. But the motivation is unwillingness to be different. It's self-love. And self-love is self-worship, personal God-defiance.

Added numbers of other Christians behaving similarly tip the scales. The Church abandons its role, mocking the Spirit's resistance of the spiritual side of escalating evil in society (and/or government). We haven't disbelieved any of the right things we had believed. But lacking power to stand for what we believe leaves us lying to the Spirit, abusing him, resisting him, grieving him, and quenching him to our peril.

What is the peril? It takes several forms. We lack authenticity. We pose no threat to forces Jesus defeated but that have not conceded defeat. They mock Jesus' enthronement over them. Worst, we partner with them in the mockery. Our testimony dims. What does God say?

Chapter 14
Inauthentic Religious

A mark of inoffensive churches is media-likeness, namely, spectacular and sensational, catchy and flashy, etc, events or programs. But a doing identity allies them to God-defiant forces. God emphasizes a being identity instead. For example inviting the Church to resist outraged God-defiance presupposes that the Church is resistance. And the Church is resistance if it stays under the leadership of the Spirit and in partnership with him.

The Church-Spirit Partnership

A passage cited earlier puts it like this.

> Do not let anyone deceive you in any way, for the day will not come until the rebellion occurs and the man of lawlessness is revealed, the man doomed to destruction. He will oppose and exalt himself over everything that is called God or is worshipped, so that he sets himself up in God's temple, proclaiming himself to be God.
>
> Now you know what [the Church] is holding him back, so that he may be revealed at the proper time. For the secret power of lawlessness is already at work, but the one

> [Holy Spirit] who now holds it back will continue to do so till he is taken out of the way.
>
> The coming of the lawless one will be in accordance with the work of Satan displayed in all kinds of misleading miracles, signs and wonders and in every sort of evil that deceives those who are perishing. They perish because they refused to love the truth and so be saved[1].

There, is the Spirit-Church partnership. As the Spirit resists invisible dimension of the power of lawlessness the Church does the visible. Visible expressions of the Church, churches, do that partly through intercessory prayer. As said earlier, those prayers help the government to be God's servant (see above).

> I urge you, first of all, to pray for all people. As you make your requests, plead for God's mercy upon them, and give thanks. Pray this way for kings and all others who are in authority, so that we can live in peace and quietness, in godliness and dignity. This is good and pleases God our Savior[2].

Look at this spin. The churches pray for rulers. Jesus and the Spirit pray for the saints[3], supposed Spirit-filled people, who make up the churches. The Scriptures don't tell us why. But they tell us supposed

Spirit-filled people can lie to the Spirit, abuse him, resist him, grieve him and quench him[4].

Christ-less Christians

The Scriptures go on to show us ways in which churches abandon their calling. Worst, they become worldly. Recall Jesus' letters to the churches in Asia Minor[5]. The church in Ephesus traded God for orthodoxy and legalism[6]. The churches in Pergamum and Thyatira[7] succumbed to false teachers and false teaching. The church in Sardis veneered lifelessness with vitality[8]. And the church in Laodicea[9] replaced spiritual wellbeing with material wellbeing.

Recovery

Tragically, each of those churches remained convinced that they knew God and God's will. They were doing it. And God was pleased with them. How did that happen? Jude tells us. All it takes is for Christ-less Christians to infiltrate pew or pulpit or both.

According to Jude, Christ-less Christians are

> ungodly; shameless; grumblers and complainers; loudmouthed braggarts; doubly dead; like roving rainless clouds; like wandering stars; like fruitless fruit-trees in harvest-time; like wild waves of the sea churning up the dirty foam of their shameless deeds.

> They, pervert the grace of Jesus Christ, and deny him; claim authority from their dreams; live immorally; scoff at evil angels [denying their existence]; defy and resist authority like Korah did Moses; mock and curse things they don't understand;
>
> Like animals they do whatever their instincts tell them; care only for themselves; flatter others to get favors in return; create divisions among believers; promise much but produce nothing; follow Cain's example who killed his brother, Abel; like Balaam, they'll do anything for money;
>
> They live by natural instinct because they don't have God's Spirit living in them; they bring about their own destruction;[10].

The churches in Ephesus, Pergamum, Thyatira, Sardis and Laodicea (see above) illustrate. It matters not whether Christ-less Christians fill the pew or pulpit. The effects are the same. Visible expressions of the Church, the churches, abandon their calling. They, bodies of supposed Spirit-filled people, lie to the Spirit, abuse him, resist him, grieve him and quench him.

That betrays the Spirit. He resists the invisible dimension of the power and spirit of lawlessness[11]. But instead of resisting the visible dimension, the churches go flirting with it. They wrench the last word from God, God's word and God's Spirit. They're back in union with satanic principles of defiance, force, greed, selfishness and evil ambition[12].

Bonanza for God-defiant forces. Free to indulge, Satan intensifies blinding people to freedom from the grip and ravages of the principles of defiance, force, greed, selfishness and evil ambition[13]. Socio-cultural and economic institutions become bolder and wilder in enticing and rewarding sensuous pleasure[14].

People who live on the approval and rewards of principles of defiance, force, greed, selfishness and evil ambition indulge. The churches can't withstand the resulting onslaught for obvious reason. They're part of the causes of the onslaught, and they're willing victims to the onslaught[15]. It's grim indeed when Christ-less Christians fill the pew or pulpit or both. But they don't have the last word. Listen to Jude's counsel to the saints.

To the saints he said. Continue to mature in your faith; pray in the Spirit; live in love; and live in expectancy for Christ's return[16]. Remember not to scorn Christ-less Christians. Be merciful to them. Snatch the snatch-able with caution lest you get sucked into their God-defiance[17]. Finally, live trusting and depending on God. He alone can keep you safe through Jesus to the end[18].

Jude's counsel parallels Jesus' command to the seven churches. He commanded them to remember, repent, and return[19]. What were they to remember, repent of and return to? Jesus told them in how he addressed himself to each church, and in how he declared himself to each church. "I know," he said.

Capsulated, the churches were to remember their former wholehearted commitment to Jesus, the LORD God, who incarnated; died to redeem lost humanity; resurrected and ascended to heaven; and was enthroned over all rule and authority, power and dominion; Lord of the Church[20].

They should remember their wholehearted love for Jesus as Lord. Their love for him was strong and hot. It defied persecution. Some of their members resisted persecution with their lives. That didn't weaken the faith and commitment of survivors. Satan knew it. The Mediterranean world knew it[21].

The churches should remember their sacrificial love for one another, and their selfless love for those who treated them like dirt. In addition, they should remember their fearless witness about the resurrection and enthronement of Jesus. How like their founding fathers, Paul and the other apostles, they resounded the good news, saturating entire districts with the love and life of Jesus[22].

How could they forget that so soon? How could they abandon all that so quickly? But they did. They tolerated Christ-less Christians who infiltrated their pews or pulpits or both (see Jude above). So what were the churches to repent of? Jesus commanded them to repent for tossing winsome life in the Spirit, and settling for repulsive life in the flesh, in oneness with the God-defiance around them[23].

The churches should mourn the folly. Weep. Confess and toss the folly. Compare James' counsel.

> Submit yourselves [afresh] to God. Resist the Devil and he will flee from you. Draw near to God and he will draw near to you. Cleanse your hands, you sinners, and purify your hearts, [double-minded people]. Be wretched and mourn and weep. Let your laughter be turned to mourning and your joy to dejection. Humble yourselves before the Lord and he will exalt you[24].

Next Jesus commanded the churches to return to their real identity, offensive identity. It was mutilated through neglect and scorn. But it survived. Return to it, Jesus ordered. Did they?

Chapter 15
Authentic Religious

Who wouldn't jump for an undeserved second chance; particularly when the offer comes from God, to give up inoffensive Christianity and return to the offensive? The churches returned. They fell in love with Jesus afresh. They renewed wholehearted commitment to

- Jesus' enthronement
- The Spirit's leadership
- The word's nurture.

Jesus' enthronement

The churches in Ephesus, Pergamum, Thyatira, Sardis and Laodicea, like those in Smyrna and Philadelphia[1], returned to Jesus as they had known him. He is enthroned over all rule and authority, power and dominion. And he is Lord of the Church[2]. They re-committed to celebrating his enthronement. How?

He had freed them from the grip and ravages of satanic principles of defiance, force, greed, selfishness, and evil ambition[3]. They lived freed from them. They defied God-defiant governments and God-defiant societies seducing and enticing them (respectively) to live for the approval and rewards of those principles. They showed contentment in letting God, God's word and God's Spirit have the last word on good and bad, right and wrong, and true and false.

He had freed them from the grip and ravages of the world's divisions and hate, fear and suspicion, etc[4]. They lived freed from them. They modeled forgiveness, compassion, kindness and reconciliation. They also modeled newness in Christ and unity in diversity[5].

He had given them the good news[6]. They lived it and told it. Conversions occurred. Transforming into Christ-likeness, saying yes to God, God's word, God's Spirit, evidenced it[7].

Once again the churches rocked the kingdom of Satan, evil angels and demons; and God-defiant governments and societies, through righteous living, and through exodus of victims from the control of God-defiance[8]. Outraged, the God-defiance fought back. But the churches were anchored in the Spirit and the word.

The Spirit's leadership

Return to Jesus' enthronement goes hand-in-hand with return to the leadership of the Spirit and renewed love, understanding and zest to obey God's word. Here was the Spirit the churches had lied to, abused, resisted, grieved and quenched. Like Samson had done to Delilah and her people[9] they had prostituted themselves to the visible reality of the antichrist, mocking the Spirit's resistance of his invisible reality[10].

But now, the churches were back in willing submission to the Spirit's leadership. Would he not comfort and empower them afresh with love and gifts? He did. Once again the churches oozed with wholehearted love for God[11]; with understanding and sympathy, other-centeredness and winsomeness[12]; with selfless love for people who treated them like dirt[13].

The Spirit gave and supervised his gifts. Using them under his direct supervision, they impacted each other and the whole—the body of all believers. The churches grew in peace and strength, knowing and reflecting Christ better and better[14]. The Church was back in submission to the Spirit's leadership and in partnership with him.

The word's nurture

The churches' return to Jesus and the Spirit meant zestful return to Jesus' word. That gladdened the Spirit. After all he inspired the word. "No prophecy of scripture is a matter of one's own interpretation, because no prophecy ever came by the impulse of man, but men moved by the Holy Spirit spoke from God"[15].

Renewed understanding stimulated renewed obedience. Zestful obedience jettisoned confidence in myths on the one hand (see above) and hollowed insights, principles, formulas, keys, etc on the other hand (see inoffensive churches above). Orthodoxy and legalism, false teaching and deception, melted. Renewed love for Jesus and the word and living in the Spirit danced in their place.

That was AD 95. The churches heeded Jesus' command. They recalled lost identity. They mourned their inoffensiveness. And they returned to Jesus as Lord, the Spirit as teacher and leader, and the word for comfort, nurture and guidance. In that way the Church leaped out of its Mediterranean base. By AD 500, according to Kenneth S. LaTourette[16], the Church had reached Ireland and Sri Lanka.

When inoffensive churches re-appear in our day we know a likely source, infiltration of Christ-less Christians. We know likely outcomes, Christianized prostitution to God-defiant governments and God-defiant societies; and humanized satanic and demonic overrun. But we also know the way out. It's wholehearted return to Jesus, the Spirit and God's word to become authentic and offensive once again. This is the cure. What is the long haul preventive? Why?

Chapter 16
Occultic

Infiltration

It's not only Christ-less Christians who infiltrate churches. Witches, satanists and spiritists (all of who I call occultists here) also do. In October 1985, I picked up in Pasadena, California a copy of a letter Diana, a high ranking occultist wrote counseling local witches on how to infiltrate churches. "A Sunday or two before you go to a church," Diana said, "walk by and see how members dress and dress like them. Do they carry a Bible, carry one. Do they wear a sickly smile, wear one. That's how you blend in."

Anton LaVey, high priest of Satan resident in San Francisco added. "Infiltrations are effective because they use Satan's easily accepted traits—deception and disguise"[1]. LaVey and Diana are telling us what we already know. Satan is most dangerous when he masquerades like an angel of light[2].

Was that how Jezebel entered the church in Thyatira[3]? How did she become influential? She lured leadership and membership into ritualistic prostitution and adultery. The church knew it but kept silent. Why?

How about youth pastor Brian who raped several girls but denied everything when the practice leaked out? And all went quiet except the lives and families of the victims. What happened to the church as resistance? A single occultist routed it? How do we detect and resist or convert Diana's colleagues floating in and out among us; carrying a Bible or wearing a sickly smile like us?

Occult infiltration has these allies. *One, consultations:* People who consult spiritists, mediums, palm-readers, psychic counselors for esoteric insights and abilities open themselves up to occult influence, nightmares, or worse a harassing spirit, for example. *Two, associations:* Associations include casual or intimate relationships with practitioners; living in un-exorcised houses or apartments in which occultists had previously lived. Haunting invisible presence, inexplicable repeated automobile accidents, disasters at home and work, and chronic ill-health are some of the harmful effects.

Three, victimization: Powerful occultists sometimes transmit occult power to their disciples by touch, thought, or glance. Vengeful individuals lacking power to get even often hire witches to hex or kill oppressors on their behalf.

Occultists believe that sexually molesting children as a sacrifice to Satan gives them tremendous power. Before the ritualistic sacrificial act, the violator invokes a spirit on herself or himself and transmits it to the victim in the ritualistic violation process. That takes the sexual violation effects beyond psychological and emotional dimensions to the spiritual. It saddles the victim with an oppressive demon that defies psychological and medical detection and treatment, and theological explanations.

Dabblers and practitioners

Occult dabblers and practitioners contact spirits that need not possess them to influence their decisions and actions from the time of contact. Spirits contacted in occult practice or dabble stay in family lines. Ancestral involvement in the occult, becomes a gateway for spirits to innocent descendants, up to three, four or more generations[4].

Heredity

Common traits in occult heredity include psychological disorders, persistent suicidal thoughts and fits of mania; incurable physical illnesses like, blindness and deafness, and hallucinations (visual, acoustic and tactile); mediumistic and clairvoyance tendencies, compulsive murderous acts and demon possession, to name but these.

These kinds of health hazards remain chronic with dabblers, practitioners, and their descendants. Some affected descendants are willing victims. They like having what they have. But most of them remain clueless about the sources of the problems that plague their lives.

Over-all, occultism hallows the defiant, and exalts the noxious and felonious. Its essential ethic is to harm, injure, kill—do evil on purpose and enjoy it. It denies

God and mocks morality. Kings Saul, Solomon, Jeroboam I and Manasseh's recourse to occultism landed Israel and Judah in conquests and exiles[5]. But occultism hinders evangelism too.

Hindrance to evangelism

Elymas was a Jew that became an occultist. He used occultic spells to block Segius Paulus, a Roman governor, from converting to Christ. Only after Paul had discerned it and had blinded Elymas for it did Segius Paulus convert[6]. Until spiritists, Appiah 105, Kpo 95, and Kamla 75 converted to Jesus, no one knew their occult practice held Christianity hostage in a 20-mile radius in Kedame, Ghana for over 80 years (see conversion story in chapter 22).

Freedom for converted practitioners

Simon the occultist and his townspeople's conversion to Christ in Samaria[7], and occultists' conversion to Christ in Ephesus[8] insist. Converts must be taught to rid themselves of occult paraphernalia. Then they must be helped immediately to claim the fullness of the Holy Spirit. Jesus taught that both acts save them from bitter backlashes[9].

In 1988 at a conference for Christian student leaders at Mittersill, Austria, I presented a seminar on "The Holy Spirit and other spirits." Jeff talked to me afterward. "As you talked, I felt a lump rise in my belly. It climbed up, up, up and finally went out through my mouth. I nearly screamed when it got to my throat because it hurt so badly. But after the lump left, I felt peace I've never felt."

I didn't know what to make of it so I asked Jeff. "Do you have a personal relationship with Jesus Christ?"

"Of course, I do. I am the president of my school chapter of IVCF. But do you know something? I have never felt this free and joyful, ready to explode. No. Never. Perhaps the lump had to do with dabbling in the occult," Jeff disclosed.

"Tell me about it," I asked.

Jeff grew up a 4th generation Methodist. In junior high, he dabbled in the occult. He contacted a spirit guide. The last year in senior high he rededicated himself to Christ. On and off through the first three years in college, he thought and silenced the thought about the occult dabble.

Most people he talked to convinced him that he had become a believer. And that took care of it. Demons and the Holy Spirit don't cohabit. He explained to them that he was a believer before he dabbled in the occult. Even so, his Christian counselors argued that theologically speaking, he had nothing to worry about. He should just believe it was over with the occult. He had become a new creation[10].

According to Jeff, he dug a theological mass grave and buried his nagging thoughts and his spirit guide in it. But the thoughts and spirit guide resurrected with a vengeance. They became nightmarish. He exhausted all the Christian help he could find. He continued to play Christian roles. But secretly he struggled with a stubborn spirit guide. Whenever it overpowered him, he let it indulge.

"But, now," Jeff said, "I am free. Free forever. Thank you."

I led him through several related scriptural references like Deuteronomy 18:9-19, Matthew 12:43-45, Acts 19:11-20, Ephesians 5:11-19, Micah 6:6-8. Now, Jeff didn't have to muster up Herculean faith to delude himself into possessing freedom he didn't have. He also didn't have to imagine the freedom he now had. Rather, he knew it as he experienced it at the time Jesus gave it to him[11].

What tripped and trapped Jeff deceived in church is one of our biggest problems. It's our over-confident theological knowing. Comforted, we toss being knowledgeable scripturally. That leaves us with theological answers for everything, but ignorant about the right questions to ask.

We remain clueless about satanic deceptions and disguise, though 2 Corinthians 11:14 had warned us about them before Lavey did (see above). Our self-imposed ignorance makes Satan, evil angels and demons more powerful and effective at our expense. Being truly biblical on the issues warns.

The conflict waged by

- defiance, force, greed, selfishness and evil ambition
- and its variant, unwillingness to yield control to God, God's word and God's Spirit

isn't content with casualties—a compromise here and there. It seeks converts—people who would turn their back on God. Or follow him hypocritically. "They profess to know God, but they deny him by their deeds; they are detestable, disobedient, unfit for any good deed"[12].

Part 4: Battlegrounds

Chapter 17
Jesus' Battlegrounds

Biblical perspectives don't give us a neat package of an occasional warfare raging out there for select experts to stop. No. Rather, they give us a messy complex conflict raging everywhere all the time, threatening us all. In fact our "yes" is gateway. "Yes" leads to victory when given to God, God's word and God's Spirit. But given to defiance, force, greed, selfishness and evil ambition; or its variant, unwillingness to let God, God's word and God's Spirit have the last word, "yes" leads to defeat.

That makes us our worst enemy or our most powerful ally in the conflict. Jesus' experience of the conflict is most educative.

Battlegrounds, Rulebooks, and Vigilantes

Right in Jesus' everyday associations all the way to the day he ascended to heaven the conflict raged. Satan didn't pull the strings. Societal, political and religious God-defiance acted on their own. But their dabble in satanic principles of defiance, force, greed, selfishness and evil ambition served Satan's purpose. The dabble pressured Jesus to defect from God or comply with God-defiance; or suffer for refusing.

The enticement started with Satan at the start of Jesus' public ministry. He pressed Jesus to defect from God or approve and adopt for personal use societal-political-religious defiance, force, greed, selfishness and evil ambition. Jesus declined. Satan quit frontal attack. He resorted to the concealed, exploiting "yes" to defiance, force, greed, selfishness and evil ambition wherever he found it[1].

Demonic God-defiance came in handy. Unlike people, demons knew who Jesus was. They became self-appointed proclaimers of Messiah[2]. Their purpose was to suck Jesus into cheap popularity with people who were looking for a hero Messiah. But Jesus always shut them up before he exorcised them. God-defiant religious, societal, and political pressures were more vicious. They came in the form of rulebooks policed by vigilantes.

But again, Satan didn't write or police the rulebooks. Social, political and religious God-defiance did. Pharisees, Pilate and Rome, and public opinion emerged as respective vigilantes. The rulebooks worked both ways, though. In one direction, and known to vigilantes, the rulebooks pushed Jesus to abuse power and position to self-serve. But in the other direction and unknown to them, each use of the rulebooks tightened the grip and ravages of satanic principles on their users, the vigilantes.

The conflict raged in the synagogues and temple; at home and weddings; at dinners in people's homes; any time Jesus healed someone or exorcised another; anytime, anywhere Jesus loved a social reject, all the way to the cross and on the cross, taunting, "save yourself."

The Pharisees' rulebook demanded that Jesus must not, heal on the Sabbath; eat with unwashed hands; teach people without a degree in theology; touch lepers; hang out with prostitutes; dine with tax collectors; raise the dead; claim to be bigger than Abraham or Moses; claim intimate knowledge of God, etc.

But Jesus defied them each time. For example, he made Matthew, a tax collector, an apostle. He dined with Zacchaeus, a chief tax collector, and saved him. He talked to a Samaritan woman at Jacob's well at Sychar, saved her and saved many Samaritans through her. He healed on the Sabbath, in the synagogues, anytime, anywhere. So the Pharisees killed Jesus because he rejected their rulebook. The charge on which they killed him was that he being human claimed to be God[3].

But Jesus' siblings too had a rulebook for him. They demanded that Jesus worked miracles at Mary's pleasure; set up a signs and wonders' seminary in Jerusalem to draw the crowds after him to the family's credit; have his work schedule approved by the family. But Jesus refused. Not only that, he called everyone who obeyed God a brother, sister and mother[4]. Outrageous. His siblings refused to believe in him[5].

Peter and his colleagues also had a rulebook for Jesus. It demanded that Jesus limited his followers to men only, no women; adults only, no kids; Jews only, no Samaritans, Greeks or Romans. How obnoxious that Jesus made them spend two nights in Sychar, Samaria while he taught newly converted Samaritans. On the resurrection morning, Mary Magdalene was first to see him. He sent her to tell Peter and others to meet him in Galilee[6]. He rejected their rulebook.

Public opinion, symbolizing God-defiant society, flipped flopped when Jesus refused to obey its rulebook. It demanded that Jesus freed Israel from Roman rule. Set up latter day Jewish kingdom to rule the world. And fill his cabinet with Jews. So they hailed him king when he entered Jerusalem riding a donkey. But when he wouldn't zap Pilate, they screamed, "Crucify him, crucify him,"[7].

Pilate symbolized the God-defiant governmental or political. He told Jesus that he had authority to crucify or free him. Jesus told him the only authority he had was the one God gave him, to be God's servant of justice and law and order. Contrary to that Pilate denied Jesus justice. He sentenced him to death by crucifixion after he had said three times that he found Jesus innocent of all the charges brought against him[8].

How strange. Moments before he ascended to heaven Jesus' disciples asked him to give them the time line for setting up a latter day Jewish kingdom. In spite of all he taught them? Anyhow, he promised them the coming of the Holy Spirit instead. And zoom, he was gone.

There we have Jesus' battlegrounds, right in his daily associations. There, allied spiritual and human God-defiance pressured him to defect from God or at least dabble in satanic principles of defiance, force, greed, selfishness and evil ambition. He suffered because he refused. And he died saying "yes" to God, God's word and God's Spirit.

The battlegrounds, rulebooks and vigilantes in Jesus' conflict foreshadowed the ones his followers must expect. And how he resisted and overcame in the conflict epitomized their resistance and overcome. Why? They face conflict at all because of their association with Jesus and loyalty to him.

Chapter 18
Disciples' Battlegrounds

"You really think God wants us to obey you rather than God? No, we would rather die a thousand times than stop talking about our personal experience of Jesus," the apostles said defying the Sanhedrin that killed Jesus[1]. How bold. Here were people who deserted Jesus at his arrest. Felt disappointed in Jesus for shattering their dreams for serving in his cabinet of a latter day Jewish kingdom. What made the difference?

The coming of the Holy Spirit did. He transformed and empowered them as Jesus had promised[2]. Like Jesus, they too became offensive and dangerous. To who? Satan and all other God-defiant authority figures and symbols. Respectively, the Sanhedrin, Judaisers, and the Caesars, emerged as vigilantes of religious, societal and political God-defiance. They pressured the early followers of Jesus to defect, comply or suffer.

Rulebooks, Vigilantes and Battlegrounds

Rulebooks matched particular God-defiance. The Sanhedrin's rulebook demanded that the apostles must not make Jesus God; tell people Jesus resurrected; speak or teach in Jesus' name; heal cripples; empty the synagogues; pollute the temple with non-Jews; dabble in preaching and teaching, monopoly of the upper class[3].

Like the Sanhedrin, converted Judaisers' rulebook insisted. Jews have first rights in Jesus; Moses plus Jesus plus adherence to Jewish circumcision rite and dietary laws equals salvation for Samaritans, Romans and Greeks; but Jews must stay out of non-Jewish homes, never eat with them[4]. Unconverted Judaisers[5] insisted, kill any Jew who admitted non-Jews to Jewish commonwealth outside Moses (the Law) and Abraham (ancestry).

God-defiance among Abraham's descendants attracted God-defiance among non-Abrahamites, Rome and the Caesars. The Caesars became gods. They demanded worship. Comply or die[6]. Again Satan didn't have to coordinate God-defiance or its varied vigilantes. They had enough inertia. It derived from personalized or institutionalized satanic principles of defiance, force, greed, selfishness or evil ambition; or its variant unwillingness to let God, God's word, and God's Spirit have the last word.

Thus the vigilantes stalked Jesus' early followers to the death at dinner in homes; prayer meetings; group Bible studies; open-air meetings; in the streets and in the temple; Damascus; Antioch; Lystra, Galatia, Caesarea, Rome and Alexandria.

That I sit here writing this book 2005 years later is evidence that those early followers of Jesus defied all threat to shut up. Philip held his life in his hand to stop in Samaria, while running from persecution in Jerusalem. He preached and converted Simon the renowned occultist and his townspeople to Jesus[7]. Peter went to Cornelius, a Roman. He saw and heard the Holy Spirit come on Cornelius and other Romans just like he had seen and heard him come on Jews, including himself, on the day of Pentecost[8].

Barnabas and Paul, John Mark and Silas, didn't only go to Romans (Sergius Paulus[9]), Greeks (Damaris and Dionysious[10]) and converted them. They partnered with them in unity and diversity to further the good news of Jesus. Lydia and Luke, Timothy and Titus, Priscilla and Aquila and Apollos[11] emerged to keep the cycle alive. At what price? Death for saying no to defiance, force, greed, selfishness and evil ambition, while saying yes to God, God's word and God's Spirit.

For example, Stephen died, stoned to death in Jerusalem; James, the brother of John, died by Herod's sword; and Matthias died, tied to a cross and eaten by vultures. Thaddeus died, crucified and shot to death by arrows; Nathaniel died, skinned alive and crucified; Philip died, hanged in the temple; and Andrew died, crucified in Egypt.

Matthew died, beheaded in Alexandria; Mark died, dragged to death behind a chariot; James (the brother of Jesus) died, thrown down from a rooftop; and Thomas died, mob-killed. Simon, the Zealot, died, sawn to pieces alive; and Paul died, beheaded on the Appianway. Before Peter died, crucified head downward, he was forced to watch his wife crucified. And Luke died, crucified in Achaia[12].

The good news of Jesus rafted rivers of blood and reached us in our societies today. The rivers scream. This is innocent blood shed on refusal to let defiance, force, greed, selfishness and evil ambition have the last word. It spilled giving the last word to God, God's word and God's Spirit.

Nothing in Scripture says that the three-pronged God-defiance, (the social, political, theological correctness and corresponding vigilantes) ended. It can't be when the satanic and demonic are rampant in all forms everywhere. According to Jesus persecution is mark of discipleship.

> Blessed are you when men revile you and persecute you and utter all kinds of evil against you falsely on my account. Rejoice and be glad, for your reward is great in heaven, for so men persecuted the prophets who were before you[13].

> Indeed all who desire to live a godly life in Christ Jesus will be persecuted[14].

> If you are reproached for the name of Christ, you are blessed, because the spirit of glory and of God rests upon you[15].

> O Sovereign Lord, how long before thou wilt judge and avenge our blood on those who dwell upon the earth? [the martyrs cried]…[in response] they were each given a white robe and told to rest a little longer, until the number of their fellow servants and their brethren should be complete, who were to be killed as they themselves had been[16].

From biblical perspectives, then, denying the conflict ignores it. But ignoring it doesn't avoid it. Rather, ignoring the conflict makes us willing victims in it.

Chapter 19
Current Battlegrounds

Vigilantes, Rulebooks, and Battlegrounds

"Yes" is all it takes to take sides in the conflict. The persecuted say yes to God, God's word and God's Spirit on good and bad, right and wrong, and true and false. On the other hand, the un-persecuted say yes to satanic principles of defiance, force, greed, selfishness, and evil ambition.

Unsung heroes form a large part of the persecuted. Like all of us they too know the reality of the surveillance of invisible rulebooks and invisible vigilantes in our daily associations, the battlegrounds. Like us all they too feel the edge of the resulting fear. But where for the sake of dear life many do nothing, unsung heroes risk their lives, rights, privileges and advantages for Christ.

Defying master-servant missionary approach: By 1988 Jonathan Lee's Islamic Resource and Training Center, Sheffield, England had attracted students from all over the world. Its uniqueness consists of "love, learn from, and serve" approach to Moslems. It contradicted the "take-it-or-leave-it Jesus is superior to Mohammed" approach that had recruited, sent and kept him fruitless for six years in Pakistan.

According to Jonathan, out of frustration he looked up a Pakistani who had been his colleague at Oxford,

England. And he invited him to tennis. While at tennis, Jonathan asked "How do you see us when we (British) come to you as missionaries?"

"Do you want to know?" his colleague asked.

"Yes" Jonathan answered.

"Do you really want to know?"

"Of course I do want to know."

"Treat us with a little respect. And love us as Jesus would" Jonathan's colleague said.

"Thanks," Jonathan said.

Jonathan didn't doubt his former colleague. But he researched the "love" and "respect" motifs further. He picked up a widespread consensus. Deeply disturbed but thankful, he wrote a paper on his findings. He invited himself to discuss it with his boss, proposing the "love, learn from and serve" approach. It backfired.

His boss said, "This is the way it has been. And this is the way it'll be. Comply or get out."

Jonathan got out. He studied, researched, prayed, and compiled material on Islam. And he opened the Islamic Resource and Training Center. Four years later, his Center became the sole trainer of his former mission's missionaries to Islamic countries.

In 1972, Donald Banks, a British journalist, went to Ghana to set up a Christian publishing company. Defying popular "master-servant" missionary approach Donald adopted a "work with, learn from and contribute to" approach. In the process, Donald picked up Richard Crabb's name. Richard had a bachelor's degree in Biochemistry and had just started working with a Government Chemical Laboratory in Accra. But writing and publishing were his first love. Donald recruited him and sent him to Wheaton Graduate School, Wheaton, Illinois for further education.

He introduced Richard to American, Canadian, Australian and British Christian publishers and booksellers' conferences and networks. Then he appointed Richard to succeed him as President of Africa Christian Press, Achimota. For the next twenty-three years, Richard published books that reached Tunisia, Iran, Fiji, Vanuatu and Papua New Guinea.

Another, that Wednesday in April 1980 Sue and Al celebrated their sixth anniversary as missionaries in rural Ghana, at a husband and wife's once a week outing. Sue told Al she wanted to child-sit for Antoinette their housekeeper so she and her husband, Ken, could also enjoy a night out. It surprised Al that Sue would think of something like that. Current missionary culture forbad missionaries to menially serve those who served them.

So Al objected. Sue refused to back down. They quarreled. But eventually Al gave in. Sue went to Ken and Antoinette's house and child-sat for them. The act made front-page headline in The Daily Graphic, Ghana's leading newspaper, "The Served Serve the Server."

Everyone wanted to meet the missionary wife and mom who risked everything to serve her servant. The result, many converted to Christ. Sue's defiance and humility lit a torch that burned in rural Ghana for years. It also ended Sue and Al's six years' no-soul-for-Christ reality.

Defying Political Ideological Crack-down to Show Love: Louisa Hopfuer became a widow in 1974. Weekly for the next 15 years, she served, on average, 30 international students to a homemade meal in her apartment in Leipzig, (East) Germany. She picked up the students and dropped them back at Karl Marx University two at a time. At the time, a car full of people other than family was suspect subject to police interception, inspection and interrogation.

Several students including a Mongolian knew Jesus personally for the first time at those hospitality meetings. A Ghanaian medical student at Karl Marx, Shome Shandorf, introduced me to Louisa in 1989. I had the privilege of introducing Louisa to Hartmut Zopf at Leipzig, barely two weeks before the wall fell. Hartmut ran students' discussion groups on ethics, using the Bible, on university campuses including Karl Marx University. Many German college students converted to Jesus through those meetings.

Then in 1989 Henry Madeva, Zimbabwe, studied for a masters' degree in Engineering in a university in Kiev, Soviet Union (now Georgia). To work around the school rule that required a written and signed permit and the presence of an assigned authority figure at a meeting that exceeded ten students, Henry pegged his numbers at nine.

But he defied the school rule that forbad evangelism. He ran an evangelistic Bible study in his room. The defiance leaked out. He was warned and threatened with deportation. He quit temporarily but resumed because eager seekers wouldn't let him. One night a 2x6-foot sliding glass window to Henry's room on the third floor of the dorm came crashing down. Someone threw a stone at it from the ground.

In no time campus military police were there. Henry was arrested and jailed on campus, charged with misdemeanor. He was released the next day at noon when he agreed to pay for labor and replacement of the glass window. The meetings continued. Student spies reported it again.

In a dark walkway between hedges a mob waylaid Henry, beat him and left him half dead. As the mob walked away, Henry said in Russian, "Lord, forgive them for they don't know what they're doing." A voice in the dark asked him to repeat what he said. He did. It was one of the campus policemen. He lifted Henry up and prop-carried him to his office. He nursed him and escorted him to his room.

That weekend the policeman was off duty. He invited Henry over, introduced him to his wife and kids and had dinner with him. Later he introduced Henry to the pastor of his underground church. The pastor gave Henry the pulpit for a month. He became a regular preacher there. Four other churches invited him to preach. And for the next three years, Henry preached and taught the Bible in five underground churches, and on campus undisturbed.

When he graduated each of the five churches wanted him for a pastor. He pastored one and taught the Bible in the others. The bonus, his church gave him a wife.

Defying Institutional Policy: Ebenezer Afful, Ghana, received both the Hebrew and Greek awards in 1981 when he graduated at Reformed Theological Seminary, Jackson, MS. But for Willem Van Gemeren, professor of Hebrew and Old Testament, who defied the current policy and made him his TA, Ebenezer would have worked on the grounds for an international student job. From RTS, Ebenezer did his PhD in Semitic Languages at Johns Hopkins, Baltimore, MD.

Defying proneness to be eternally secure financially: Gary is an Accountant, a husband, and father of a son four, and a daughter two. Recently he gave up a job that paid $100,000 to take another that paid $35,000. The family relocated to a poorer neighborhood and changed lifestyle accordingly. Gary's former job made him compromise Jesus. It also left him no time for wife and family. The latter gave him time to lead a home group, and be with family and wife.

In 1988 Michael Mungodo, Tanzania, was a husband, a father of two kids aged three and five, and a PhD Engineering student, in Moscow, Soviet Union (now Russia). He and his wife used a year's savings to buy a winter coat for a Papua New Guinean colleague who couldn't afford a windbreaker. In the store, before he wore the coat the Papua New Guinean asked, "Michael, why are you doing this? You don't even know me."

Michael said, "My wife and I have experienced the love of Jesus. So, please give us the privilege and pleasure to share his love with you."

"Tell me about him," the Papua New Guinean said.

Michael told him his own faith story, how he came to know Jesus personally. He asked him to trust Jesus to save him. And he too would have a faith story to tell others. He did. Michael discipled him. He chose the name John when he asked for baptism. Both Michael and John graduated two years later. These were John's words to Michael before they parted company in Moscow. "I go home as a missionary to my people. I'll keep in touch. Thanks for leading me to Jesus."

Defying personal "taboo" to serve others: Heidi and Harry are real estate agents. They are opposed to gay marriages. But in 2004 they served a gay couple as they do any other clients. A month after the couple had moved into their new home they sent a thank you card to Heidi and Harry. It read, "Dear Heidi and Harry, how can we thank you enough? You were the only local realtors willing to help us buy a house. We want you to know we love you dearly and respect you highly. Drop any literature on Jesus any time; Love."

Imagined socially correct, politically correct and theologically correct vigilantes are scarier and more powerful than the actual. Because imagining them, immortalizes them. They become all-present and all-powerful. They co-habit our living space. That close they see and hear every violation. They thunder "defect or comply or suffer."

The thunder sends the shivers, conjuring images of the pain of ridicule or ostracism; loss of reputation or certain rights, or privileges or advantages. We freeze in fear. We quench the desire to stand for what we believe. Frozen, we glide past opportunities to show

- our love for God and people[1]
- our commitment to unity in diversity[2]
- our zeal to be witnesses for Jesus[3], etc.

What do we do instead? We contradict ourselves. In our hearts and minds we say yes to God, God's word and God's Spirit; and no to defiance, force, greed, selfishness and evil ambition. But in our actions we say yes to defiance, force, greed, selfishness and evil ambition; and no to God, God's word and God's Spirit. But contradiction is a lie.

So in lying to ourselves, we lie to the Spirit and abuse him; we take his mercy for granted. We resist him, grieve him and quench him. What a price. How did the unsung heroes cited above and numerous others, and early followers of Jesus make it in the conflict? How did Jesus? How would we resist and overcome in the conflict?

Part 5: Resistance

Chapter 20
Jesus' Model of Resistance

Jesus hanged on the cross in a mangled body, the work of Satan and people (the Pharisees, Pilate and Rome). He anticipated the "work" that

- only God must do
- only God must see
- only God must approve[1].

The unrelenting pressure came crashing three concentric circles of people to reach Jesus.

The Pharisees formed the outermost circle. The soldiers formed the inner. And one of the crucified criminals formed the innermost, closest to Jesus' ear. The all-time pressure to defect from God buzzed "If you are the Son of God, save yourself"[2].

His persistent yes to the Father had brought him this far. In a moment the Father would punish sin personified in the sinless one, Jesus, God incarnate. The moment Jesus himself had dreaded but had said yes to is imminent[3]. In comparison, the physical—human—torture and disfigurement looked pale.

How tempting to defect this close to the climactic. But Jesus refused to defect. Darkness dimmed noontime sunlight for three hours. During that time God the Father did to Jesus what only he must do, see and approve as punishment for human sin. Done, the darkness lifted. "It's finished," accomplished, Jesus said. And he died[4].

The grave was formality. Jesus resurrected and ascended to heaven. The Father enthroned him over all rule and authority, power and dominion[5]. Jesus faced the "yes" conflict everyday of his life. How did he make it through a conflict of land-mines? How did he model resistance and overcome so his followers, including you and me, can copy him?

The Pharisees; Satan and demons; public opinion; Herod, Pilate and Rome; Jesus' disciples; Jesus' siblings; and Jesus' knowledge of having to take God's wrath for sin, all pressured Jesus everywhere all the time to say yes to God-defiance and no to God, God's word and God's Spirit. Jesus outmatched the daily conflict with lifestyle resistance made up of the Spirit, love, self-imposed weakness, and prayer.

The Spirit

Jesus lived in and by the Spirit of God. He was incarnated in and by the Spirit. "The Holy Spirit will come upon you," the angel told Mary. "And the power of the Most High will overshadow you; therefore the child to be born will be called holy the Son of God"[6].

Jesus did his public ministry in the Spirit, who came on Jesus at his baptism[7]. "The Spirit of the Lord is upon me" to preach the good news of the kingdom of God, Jesus said[8]. Even for Jesus, God insisted, "Not by might, nor by power, but by my Spirit, says the LORD of hosts"[9].

Unlike us Jesus knew and could do the Father's will at the right time and place. He is always God. But like us he too submitted to being empowered and led moment by moment by the Spirit. When the Pharisees credited demons instead for that empowerment, Jesus told them they sinned against the Spirit. Such sins have no forgiveness, ever[10].

Love

In addition to living in and by the Spirit, Jesus lived love. He demonstrated his love for the Father through obedience to him. He said and did only what he'd heard and seen the Father say and do[11]. Then he said that the Father hung out with him because he always did what pleased the Father[12].

That included submission to Satan's power, "the power of darkness"[13]; the temple officers' verbal and physical abuse, the Sanhedrin's mock-trial, and Pilate's unjust trial and sentence[14]. But Jesus also loved people.

In a moment Jesus would raise Lazarus from the grave. Mary didn't know that. So she wept for the death of her brother. Jesus wept when he saw her weeping[15]. Onlookers said, "See how he [Jesus] loved him [Lazarus]"[16]. Moved by compassion, Jesus touched and healed a leper, a social taboo[17]. Then Jesus invited himself to dinner with Zacchaeus, a chief tax collector, a social reject[18]. At dinner in a Pharisee's home, Jesus let a prostitute, another social reject, touch him[19].

Behaviors of that kind made his enemies nickname him the friend of sinners. But Jesus loved his enemies as well. He wept over Jerusalem, the city he held responsible for killing all the prophets[20]. He prayed forgiveness for those who crucified him[21]. Jesus loved us, sinners, to save us from the wrath of God. "Greater love has no man than this, that a man lay down his life for his friends"[22].

So Jesus taught and modeled love. And he insists that love should distinguish his disciples. Love is the product of saying "yes" to God, God's word and God's Spirit. It cuts across the world's divisions, hate and violence that derive from satanic principles of defiance, force, greed, selfishness and evil ambition[23].

Self-imposed Limitation

Succinctly, Philippians 2:1-11 says Jesus served the Father through self-imposed weakness. Meaning Jesus gave up his right to be God[24]. To the extent, he depended on the Father and obeyed him as a servant, though he's co-equal with him[25]. He put it like this:

> I tell you the truth, the Son can do nothing by himself; he can do only what he sees his Father doing, because what the Father does the Son also does...By myself I can do nothing; I judge only as I hear, my judgment is just, for I seek not to please myself but him who sent me[26].

For I have come down from heaven not to do my will but to do the will of him who sent me[27].

My teaching is not my own. It comes from him who sent me. If anyone chooses to do God's will, he will find out whether my teaching comes form God or whether I speak on my own[28].

When you have [crucified] the Son of Man, then you will know that I am the one I claim to be, and that I do nothing on my own but speak just what the Father has taught me. The one who sent me is with me; he has not left me alone, for I always do what pleases him[29].

For, I did not speak on my own accord, but the Father who sent me commanded me what to say and how to say it. I know that his command leads to eternal life. So whatever I say is just what the Father has told me to say[30].

Prayer

Further, Jesus showed his perfect submission to the Father through prayer. He had said he wouldn't use his power recklessly[31]. He had committed to serving God as a servant[32]. He prayed daily not to switch. Faced with premature death threats Jesus prayed and depended on the Father to rescue him when and how he deemed fit (see chapter 2).

> In the days of his flesh, Jesus offered up prayers and supplications, with loud cries and tears, to him who was able to save him from death, and he was heard for his godly fear. Although he was a Son, he learned obedience through what he suffered;[33].

That says Jesus didn't just pray or pray only in crisis. No. Jesus prayed revering the Father. And that was the basis on which the Father answered him. In addition Jesus prayed as if his life depended on prayer. Sometimes he prayed at dawn. Other times he spent whole nights praying. He prayed a whole night prior to choosing the twelve, among them, Judas who betrayed him[34].

He prayed and multiplied bread and fish to feed 5,000 and 4,000 men, discounting women and children. He prayed and raised Lazarus from the grave[35]. On the cross he prayed forgiveness for the Pharisees, Pilate, the soldiers, people who denied him justice, treated him like dirt and crucified him[36]. Jesus' disciples had seen Jesus walk on water, raise the dead, exorcise demons, etc. But they never asked him to teach them to do any of those. Rather, they asked him, "Teach us to pray"[37].

There it is. Jesus resisted in the conflict through a lifestyle of prayer, self-imposed weakness, love and the Spirit. Why? How close did his immediate followers follow his example? Why? And how close must we? Why?

Chapter 21
Disciples' Resistance

The Sanhedrin and Judaisers professed to know God. The Caesars and Rome didn't. But they all had one thing in common. Like Satan, they indulged in God-defiance. Its ultimate expression was death to the followers of Jesus, and death to the idea of Jesus as God.

Ruthless and relentless, they pushed Jesus' followers, as they had done Jesus, to defect from God and adopt God-defiance, or suffer. But like Jesus they too resisted with their lives. They lived a lifestyle made up of the Spirit; self-imposed weakness; love; and prayer to survive authentic in the conflict (see chapter 18).

The Spirit

Ten days after Jesus' ascension and enthronement, the Spirit came. He filled the followers of Jesus (120 in number) gathered in the upper room[1]. Since then, being Spirit-filled became the telling mark of being a disciple of Jesus. Comforted and empowered, taught and led, by him, the disciples said no to defiance, force, greed, selfishness and evil ambition forced on them by the Sanhedrin and Rome plus translucent satanic and demonic involvement[2].

Specifically, led by the Spirit, Peter discerned and punished Ananias and Sapphira with sudden death for lying to the Spirit and abusing him[3]. Peter and John imparted the gift of the Spirit to other believers through the laying on of hands[4]. As Peter preached to Cornelius and a non-Jewish audience in his house the Spirit cut short his sermon. He filled non-Jews visibly and audibly as he had done Jews on Pentecost[5].

Led by the Spirit, Stephen showed a blend of grace and power, and wisdom and Christ-likeness. Libertarian Judaisers and the Sanhedrin failed to match his wisdom, fervor and eloquence. They lynched him by stoning[6]. But led by the Spirit, Stephen prayed forgiveness for his lynchers.

His colleague, Philip was similarly led by the Spirit. Like Jesus[7], Philip defied Jewish hatred for Samaritans. He stopped in Samaria while running from persecution in Jerusalem. He preached salvation in Jesus. He worked miraculous signs and wonders. They outmatched those done by a reigning occultist known as Simon. He and his townspeople converted to Jesus[8].

Barnabas also was full of the Holy Spirit. He led many people to Jesus as a result[9]. Led by the Spirit, Paul discerned and punished Elymas, a Jew become an occultist, with temporal blindness for blocking Sergius Paulus from converting to Jesus. Only then did Sergius convert to Christ[10]. Led by the Spirit, Paul made a cripple walk in Lystra[11], and he exorcised a demonized person at Philippi[12].

Led by the Spirit, Paul distinguished the Spirit's intervention to redirect[13], from Satan's interception to obstruct[14]. Indeed everything the disciples did was done in and by the Spirit[15].

Self-imposed weakness

Then like Jesus, his disciples showed contentment to be nobodies for his sake. John the Baptizer rejoiced to see his disciples leave him to follow Jesus[16]. Compare the Pharisees, who intensified efforts to kill Jesus for attracting their disciples[17].

For a moment, Zacchaeus forgot that he was a chief treasurer. He climbed a tree to see Jesus. Jesus invited himself to dinner in his house. Overwhelmed with Jesus' presence, Zacchaeus said, "I give half of my income to the poor. And I pay back four times people I had cheated"[18]. Un-obliged, Matthew, Peter, Paul and others gave up everything they had to follow Jesus[19].

Love

As love marked Jesus so it did his disciples. Mary Magdalene, Joanna, Susanna, and many other women gave themselves and their resources to support Jesus[21]. Lydia hosted Paul and his team[22]. Mary, the sister of Lazarus and Martha, washed Jesus' feet with oil and wiped them with her hair[23]. Out of love, Stephen prayed forgiveness for his lynchers[24].

Barnabas sold a piece of land he owned. He gave all the money to the apostles to distribute as they deemed fit[25]. He bridged Paul to the disciples when everyone was skeptical about Paul's sudden and radical conversion. Eight years later, he sought Paul out and bridged him to the church in Antioch[26]. He gave John

Mark a second chance[27]. Paul wrote 13 of the 27 books of the New Testament. Mark wrote the gospel of Mark.

Philip[27] and believers from Cyprus and Cyrene[28] crossed racial and socio-cultural lines out of love to share their personal experience of Jesus. The results were astounding. Philip's preaching converted a powerful occultist and his townspeople in Samaria. The preaching of believers from Cyprus and Cyrene converted Greeks and Romans. They formed a church of Jews, Greeks and Romans in Antioch. The Spirit endorsed the church in Antioch. From there he sent out Barnabas and Paul on cross-cultural missions[29].

At least twice, Paul said he wished to go to hell if that would save the Jews[30]. Then there were Priscilla and Aquila, husband and wife. They mentored Apollos, an itinerant evangelist, and made him more effective[31]. Priscilla and Aquila hosted Paul and many other itinerant preachers[32].

Prayer

Acts 4:23-31 says

> On their release, Peter and John went back to their own people and reported all that the chief priests and elders had said to them. When they heard this, they raised their voices together in prayer to God. "Sovereign Lord," they said, "you made the heaven and the earth and the sea, and everything in them. You spoke by the Holy

Spirit through the mouth of your servant, our father David:

"'Why do the nations rage and the people plot in vain? The kings of the earth take their stand and the rulers gather together against the Lord and against his Anointed One.'

Indeed Herod and Pontius Pilate met together with the Gentiles and the people of Israel in this city to conspire against your servant Jesus, whom you anointed. They did what your power and your will had decided beforehand should happen. Now, consider their threats and enable your servants to speak your word with great boldness. Stretch out your hand to heal and perform miracles, signs and wonders through the name of your holy servant Jesus."

After they prayed, the place where they were meeting was shaken. And they were filled with the Holy Spirit and spoke the word of God boldly.

Threatened with death by the very people who killed Jesus, the disciples prayed. They didn't pray for protection. They prayed that God strengthen them to boldly declare Jesus' resurrection and enthronement. But persecution didn't drive them to prayer. They had developed the habit, having learned from Jesus earlier[33].

Peter prayed and raised Dorcas from death[34]. Paul and Silas prayed and the prison quaked at Philippi. As a result the jailer and his household converted to Christ[35]. Paul asked other believers to pray for him[36].

Jude taught the most about Christ-less Christians (see chapter 14 above). He also taught prayer as an effective way to guard against the infiltration of Christ-less Christians[37]. The churches in Pergamum and Thyatira forgot to do that. Therefore they were overrun by false teachers, false teaching and syncretism.

That lifestyle resistance made up of prayer, love, self-imposed weakness and the Spirit worked for Jesus and his early disciples must be good news to us. Or is it a challenge? Why?

Chapter 22
Current Resistance

Bill Becker and Sally Sutton had these things in common. Bill taught systematic theology for 15 years. Sally was a pastor for 15 years. Sally and Bill respectively taught their pastorates and classrooms that the miraculous had ceased with the apostles. Their unbelief and disbelief generated hatred and anger in students and church-members that believed otherwise.

In the 16th year cancer snatched the classroom from Bill and the pulpit from Sally. When cancer started to mock medical science, Sally and Bill asked family and friends to pray for miraculous healing. Bill and Sally died in a year. Conclusions differed among people who knew them.

Some said God called his servants home. Others blamed Satan instead. He cut short Sally's life at 41 and Bill's at 43. Still others said Sally and Bill's unbelief and disbelief killed them. Medical treatment, faith and prayer would have healed them. But to blame-shift or scapegoat, rationalize or debate here misses the point.

For wherever unbelief and disbelief, and hatred and anger polarize Christians both sides say no to God, God's word and God's Spirit; and yes to defiance, force, greed, selfishness and evil ambition. Humility and openness elude one side, and compassion and forgiveness elude the other to Satan's delight.

Tragic, because believers' unwillingness to let God, God's word and God's Spirit have the last word on good and bad, right and wrong, true and false[1] ties them to

- people who live on the approval and rewards of principles of defiance, force, greed, selfishness and evil ambition[2]
- socio-cultural, economic, civil, political and religious institutions that insist on being the last word on good and bad, right and wrong, true and false[3]
- Satan who blinds people to freedom from the grip and ravages of the principles of defiance, force, greed, selfishness and evil ambition[4]

The resulting situation is evil overrun in which believers in Jesus are willing victims[5]. To redress, Jude had called for a return to lifestyle resistance.

Continue to mature in your faith, he said. Pray in the Spirit; live in love; and live in expectancy for Christ's return[6]. Remember not to scorn Christ-less Christians. Be merciful to them. Snatch the snatch-able with caution lest you get sucked into their ways[7]. Finally, live trusting and depending on God. He alone can keep you safe through Jesus to the end[8].

Capsulated, lifestyle resistance consists of the Spirit, self-imposed weakness, love and prayer. Jesus lived it to resist and overcome in the conflict (see chapter 20). His early disciples did (see chapter 21).

So must we to survive authentic in the conflict and be effective. Why?

The Spirit

Only the Spirit blends boldness and kindness, wisdom and humility[9] to resist

One, believer vigilantes, ready to crack-down on giving the last word to God on good and bad, right and wrong, and true and false: Jonathan is typical (see chapter 19). He lost his job for suggesting that his mission substitute "love, learn from, serve" for "take-it-or-leave-it" approach in missions to Moslems. But when his former mission came four years later, running after him for his programs he agreed.

Donald and Sue (see chapter 19) acted like Jonathan. Unafraid to be obnoxious to fellow missionaries, they countered "master-servant" approach to missions with "work with, menially serve, learn from and contribute to" approach. Self-evident effectiveness vindicated them. But they remained humble.

Two, vigilantes of approval and rewards of satanic principles of defiance, force, greed, selfishness and evil ambition, ready to ridicule, marginalize, and taunt violators: Friends at church, colleagues at work, neighbors and extended family members told Gary he was out of his mind to give up a $100,000 job for a $35,000 one, relocate and downsize living style accordingly. He lost relationships over that. But he kept a cool head, a sign of the Spirit's enablement (see chapter 19).

Three, God-defiant social, political, and religious, ties—vigilantes—ready to crack-down on violators: Louisa in chapter 19 is typical. She risked her life weekly for over 15 years giving a homemade meal in her apartment to 30 international students. She picked and dropped them off two at a time at Karl Marx University, Leipzig, Germany.

Similar to Louisa, Henry risked deportation or death for organizing evangelistic Bible study in his room on campus in Kiev, Georgia. Willem knew his job was on the line when, contrary to institutional policy, he made a straight "A" international student his TA in Hebrew. And Heidi and Harry knew they were under social and religious vigilantes' surveillance when they helped a gay couple buy a house.

In saying yes to God and no to collective God-defiance, Heidi and Harry; Willem; Henry; Louisa; Gary; Sue; Donald; and Jonathan desisted resisting, grieving and quenching the Spirit. Honored thus, the Spirit converted (or freed) people Satan had blinded to freedom from the grip and ravages of satanic principles of defiance, force, greed, selfishness and evil ambition. Transformed and transforming individuals and churches resulted (see chapter 19 and compare with chapter 15).

Self-imposed limitations

Why would anyone go on missions if it's not to see people convert to Jesus? Unfortunately it's easy to help or hinder the process. Sue and Al (chapter 19) and Kaye and Chris were missionaries in Ghana about the same time. As said earlier, Sue defied current "master-servant" missionary approach to missions when she child-sat for Antoinette, her housekeeper.

Unlike Sue, Kaye and Chris (and Al, Sue's husband) towed the "master-servant" line. Kaye slapped Jo, one of their cooks and housekeepers. Jo's charge, she failed to clean up a clogged master bedroom bathtub after use. At dinner that evening, Jo stood right there when 9-year old Paul, Kaye and Chris' second son, confessed. "Mom, I used your bathtub in the morning. But I didn't tell any of the housekeepers. I'm sorry." Kaye never apologized to Jo.

Sue's menial service reached front-page in a major newspaper. It attracted many people to Sue and Al. The result, many converted to Jesus. Kaye's physical abuse of Jo also traveled far and wide. It distanced people from Kaye and Chris. Why?

Kaye's physical abuse of a cook and housekeeper tied her and Chris to a hydrologist expert, who was currently in the country supervising the construction of a Dam. He occupied a wing of Hotel Continental, Accra. He was and felt high in demand, untouchable, and a law to himself. Among other things, he verbally abused hotel personnel and got away with it.

Kaye couldn't for obvious reason. The hydrologist didn't pretend to be Christian. But Kaye wasn't only Christian. She and Chris were cross-cultural missionaries. They represented Jesus. What they were and were not in attitudes and behavior Jesus was and wasn't. But how did Kaye's incident get out? How did Sue's act?

Sue's housekeeper, Antoinette, had been a schoolteacher. Her husband Ken was a pharmacist. They had a network of people. And Kaye's housekeeper, Jo, had been a self-employed baker. Peter, her husband was a communications specialist. They too had a network of people.

Sue fed Christ-likeness to Antoinette's network of people. Conversions occurred and rocked heaven ecstatic, gladdening Sue and (reluctant) Al. Kaye fed un-Christ-likeness to Jo's network of people, bad press for missionary and Jesus. No conversions occurred. But Kaye's undoing lay outside Jo's network. It lay instead in Kaye's "yes" to her master-servant network. That network forbad "masters" to be courteous, Christ-like, to "servants."

Sue freed herself and Al from six years of ineffectiveness when she said "no" to that network. Jonathan did and freed himself and many missions (including his former mission) and many missionaries from ineffectiveness. And Donald picked up Richard, a caliber of person he could meet only through working with and learning from to earn a right to contribute to (see chapter 19).

Jesus didn't only ask his representatives at home and overseas to be non-threatening (sheep), wise (snakes), and harmless (doves). He modeled what it takes. "The Son of Man came not to be served but to serve, and to give his life as a ransom for many"[10]. That makes giving up influence and authority, rights and privileges to serve people and learn from them to earn a right to contribute to a sign of love for God and people.

Love

Only after we have experienced God's love can we love God. Only that experience frees from judgmental love[11]. And only that experience frees Jesus in us to embrace Jesus in others across cultural, social, racial, political, doctrinal etc lines.

Electrified by that love Louisa refused to idle bemoaning the death of her husband of 25 years. Instead, she risked her life weekly to entertain 30 international students in her apartment for over 15 years in Leipzig, Germany (see chapter 19). Similarly, motivated by that love, Michael and his wife used a year's savings to buy a winter coat for a fellow international student in graduate school in Moscow, Russia. No wonder conversions occurred (see chapter 19, and compare Jonathan, Donald, Sue, and Henry).

Anything short of love mocks theological correctness. Jesus' charge against the church in Ephesus was exactly that. That church traded love for orthodoxy and legalism[12]. Lovelessness also mocks spiritual power[13].

Recall the church in Florida that had supported 80% of Julie's missionary budget (chapter 13). It tore down berserk spiritual forces in cities in Bulgaria on Julie's invitation. But it rejected the Bulgarian male pastor Julie chose to marry following the tearing down event. It withdrew its support.

Fortunately, Stephen demonstrated that prayer keeps the balance between grace (love) and power, and wisdom and the Spirit[14].

Prayer

With his last breath, Stephen[15] prayed forgiveness for his lynchers. Earlier Stephen's opponents failed to match the love, power, wisdom and Spirit that oozed from him[16]. Henry, a foreign graduate student in Kiev, Georgia was like Stephen (see chapter 19). He also prayed forgiveness for colleagues who mob-beat him for running evangelistic Bible studies on campus.

Through endurance and prayer, his undying love snatched a Christian military policeman from drowning in double allegiance, i.e., "yes" to ideological God-defiance to keep his job, and "yes" to God, as church member. Snatched and restored, the policeman bridged Henry to five churches to teach the Bible. As said earlier, Henry became pastor of one of them and a Bible teacher in the others.

Similarly and dissimilarly, a ten-day fast and prayer, and naïve obedience to the prompting of the Spirit, led to the conversion of three spiritists aged 105, 95 and 75. At an open-air meeting in Kedame in Ghana while a teenager, I challenged the spiritists to kill me to prove their claim to have powers superior to God's power. The next morning they confessed that they tried but ran into an impenetrable wall of fire around me.

They were convinced that was God. They decided to become Christian. Their conversion rippled into countless conversions. Christians and non-Christians from within 20-mile radius verified the spiritists' conversion, divulged protective medicines, talismans and amulets they had had from them, and trusted Jesus to save them. In a month churches within 20-mile radius swarmed with new converts as a result.

Jesus prayed all his life. Why does he continue to pray in his enthronement? And why does the Spirit join him to pray for the saints? The reality says we can't ever pray enough. We pray, not for divine intervention when all else fails (see Bill and Sally above). We pray as a way of life. Pray when it looks foolish to pray, like God and God praying to God.

Do we not need the Spirit to lead us to pray and wait, not despair or take charge, when God seems slow and weak, silent and distant, unfair and uncaring? We need the Spirit to help us trust and depend on God to come through when and how he deems fit.

Even so we want to know why a lifestyle made up of prayer, love, self-imposed limitation and the Spirit is God's way out in the conflict. We also want to know why the conflict continues.

Part 6: Rationale

Chapter 23
God-defiance

God designed God-dependence, friendship with God, to counter God-defiance, which is enmity with God. And God chose conflict; and the Spirit, self-imposed weakness, love and prayer, as the process. Why?

Why Conflict?

God could forcibly stop God-defiance. He could order Satan, evil angels and demons out of existence. And they would cease to exist (chapters 7-10). Then there wouldn't be a Satan deceiving the nations. No antichrist to come and ravage the nations and societies. The government would be the servant of God. And public goodwill will replace public evil-will, eliminating the occult (chapters 11-16).

God is God. Who can resist him? But if God forcibly stopped God-defiance, he would abuse power and position. He's the only one who has supreme power. However, if God allowed God-defiance to indulge, God-defiance wins and God loses. He loses his purpose for creation.

Sovereign but un-arbitrary, God chose conflict. In the Garden of Eden God put enmity, conflict, between Satan (representative of God-defiance) and Jesus (the giver and representative of God-dependence),[1]. He invited God-defiance to the fight to self-defend. Jesus' crucifixion mirrored how intertwined spiritual and human God-defiance has been since the conflict began (see chapters 2, 7-16).

In the crucifixion, Judas, Satan, the Sanhedrin, Pilate, sin and death[2] symbolizing spiritual and people God-defiance, gave the fight their all. What allied forces didn't know was God's wisdom behind the conflict. What was it?

Why self-imposed weakness?

Jesus gave up equality with God and chose to serve God as a servant. That was self-limitation, weakness posture, at its best[3]. But like the conflict, Jesus' self-imposed weakness looked foolish to Satan and his spiritual and people allies[4].

But because Jesus' self-imposed weakness wasn't wimpy it provoked maximum response. That was why Satan, the Pharisees, Pilate and Rome, used their deadliest and ultimate weapon, death. Christ absorbed death and turned it into life-giving victory[5]. Allied God-defiant forces lost fighting. They were defeated, not forcibly, but through self-imposed weakness.

That was God's wisdom behind the conflict and self-imposed weakness[6]. What role did the Spirit, love and prayer play?

Why the Spirit?

1 Corinthians 2:11 insists only the Spirit knows the thoughts of God. That includes God's wisdom behind

the conflict and his means of resistance and overcome in it, namely, self-imposed weakness, love, prayer and the Spirit. Jesus knew that. Therefore, though God-incarnate, he submitted to the Spirit's hovering at his baptism, and did his public ministry in the power of the Spirit[7].

Jesus must know that the Spirit would hover over his resurrection and enthronement[8] as he had done his incarnation[9]. Accordingly, Jesus taught that the Spirit would hover over transformation[10]. Facilitators of transformation would be credible and effective only under the hovering of the Spirit. Wait for his hovering, Jesus ordered[11].

Why Love?

God's love behaved like Jesus' self-imposed weakness. It looked naïve, poor war strategy, to pit love against satanic principles of defiance, force, greed, selfishness and evil ambition. Used to brute force, the God-defiant underestimated the power of love[12].

But in Jesus the power of love broke the power of unbiblical socio-cultural taboos, divisions and hate, biases and prejudices: Jesus dined with tax collectors. He let prostitutes touch him, out of compassion. In Jesus the power of love broke the power of sin and disease, and the power of demons and death: Jesus forgave sin, healed the sick, exorcised the demonized, and raised the dead, out of compassion.

In Jesus the power of love broke the power of personal God-defiance: He chose to suffer in obedience to the Father, rather than yield to pressure from Satan, the Pharisees, public opinion, etc to abuse power and position. He submitted to judicial injustice and the power of Satan to die the death of a criminal, out of love for his Father[13].

Thus through his life and teaching, Jesus showed that love is stronger than hate. He commanded his followers to be known by love[14]. But even Jesus didn't live like that without prayer.

Why prayer?

Hebrews 5:7-10 answers.

> In the days of his flesh, Jesus offered up prayers and supplications, with loud cries and tears, to him who was able to save him from death, and he was heard for his godly fear. Although he was a Son, he learned obedience through what he suffered; and being made perfect he became the source of eternal salvation to all who obey him, being designated by God a high priest after the order of Melchizedek.

There it is. God had put Jesus on the line, the conflict. He had invited Satan—symbolic of God-defiance—to the fight. Through Jesus, God would confront God-defiance (enmity with God) to establish God-dependence (friendship with God). Therefore should Jesus die a premature death, God's agenda was finished. God lost. And Satan won.

Yet, faced with repeated premature death threats (see chapters 2, 17 and 20), Jesus had to feel desperate and cry out for help. And the Father rescued him from premature death, to prevent his own agenda from being aborted. The basis of rescue and prevention, Jesus prayed and trusted and depended on the Father to rescue him when and how he deemed fit. What does that say?

The Hebrews passage continues. One, Jesus, perfected his deliberate choice to trust and depend on the Father through prayer. Two, as a result he became the source and model of God-dependent rescue, salvation. Forever, three, he remains the link between God and the saved. And four, Jesus' desperate, deliberate and dependent prayers provided a legitimate basis for God to use ultimate power.

So prayer marked Jesus' life and public ministry, all the way to the crucifixion. Just before Jesus died, he prayed again. "Father, into your hands I commit my spirit"[15]. But after Jesus' enthronement over all rule and authority, power and dominion following his resurrection and ascension[16], Jesus started praying again.

Jesus and the Spirit pray for the saints[17]. Is it because the saints face the conflict though Jesus had defeated God-defiant allied forces?

Chapter 24
God-dependence

Why Conflict?

Hallelujah. Jesus is enthroned. His enthronement is proof that God-defiance, enmity with God, is indeed defeated. God-dependence, friendship with God, is here. But for God-dependence to counter God-defiance, God-dependence must be a love relationship between God and people. It must be a relationship people enter and stay in out of freewill and love. It mustn't be forced on people or policed.

Since defeated God-defiance hasn't conceded defeat, it resists losing victims to Jesus. God-defiance goes after lost victims seeking to retrieve them. Tragically, our "yes" to God doesn't rule out the presence of residues of God-defiance in us. Provoked or intimidated, we're capable of reciprocating the aggression or acquiescing to it (see chapters 17-22). Only in the Spirit can we resist with our lives as Jesus did (see chapters 2, 17 and 20).

Why the Spirit?

Only the Spirit-led see wisdom, privilege and dignity in deliberate and conscious participation in the conflict. It is God's way to confront God-defiance. It invites God-defiance to the fight. God-defiance in all its forms (chapters 7-16) fights self-defending, and loses self-defeated (chapters 17-19). Worldly wisdom akin to God-defiance doesn't understand God's wisdom in that[1].

Only the Spirit-led see wisdom, privilege and dignity in lifestyle resistance made up of the Spirit, self-imposed weakness, love and prayer. It is God's only way out in the conflict. Lifestyle resistance is the one thing that God-defiance in all its forms (chapters 7-16) can't stand, understand, imitate or overcome (chapters 20-22).

Only the Spirit-led know the God who is Spirit better, and reflect him better.

> God is spirit, and those who worship him must worship in spirit and in truth[2]...And this is eternal life, that they know you the only true God, and Jesus Christ whom you have sent[3].

Jesus insists that only under the Spirit's leadership can we, his witnesses,

- know him in his bodily resurrected and enthroned form as we should; he is the good news and its commissioner[4]

- grasp the source of the message of the good news; it is all the Scriptures and disentangled understanding of the Scriptures[5]

- understsnd the theme of the message of the good news; it is the crucified and resurrected and enthroned Jesus according to the Scriptures, and proclamation of repentance and forgiveness in his name to the nations[6]

- be credible witnesses of the resurrected and enthroned Jesus and the good news, clothed with the Spirit as we should[7]

- ooze the fragrance of the good news; we're blessed to be a blessing to others, and we're joyful, prayerful and praiseful[8].

Only self-imposed weakness desists resisting, grieving and quenching the Spirit as he seeks to make Jesus that real in us[9].

Why self-imposed weakness?

Only in self-imposed weakness can we know better the God who defeated God-defiance in weakness and saves the weak in weakness, and reflect him better[10]. We have insatiable need for acceptance and appreciation, recognition and success, approval and rewards. Therefore only we can choose to give it up to be "nothing" a "nobody" for Jesus. In John the Baptizer's words, we dim ourselves so that Jesus will shine his greatness through us[11].

We choose to be vulnerable, frail (sheep), wise (snakes), and pure and harmless (doves)[12]. Non-threatening, non-judgmental, and winsome, we become true clay vessels, through which God's power and grace flow to weaklings needing them. Then it becomes obvious that

> What we preach is not ourselves, but Jesus Christ as Lord, with ourselves as your servants for Jesus' sake…But we have this treasure in earthen vessels, to show that the transcendent power belongs to God and not us[13].

Indeed Spirit-led self-imposed weakness is invincible and contagious (chapters 20-22). But love is the acid test.

Why love?

Only in love can we know the God who is love better and reflect him better. How else can we show our love for him except by a deliberate choice to love him above all other love ties, e.g., family and race of origin, social and professional classes, political and religious affiliations, etc[14]? How else would those ties, rivals of God, know that God is our number one love except through tasting the proof of our faithfulness to God?

Our faithfulness isn't legalism or self-styled fanaticism. No. Rather, it's red-hot devotion to the one who loved us when what we deserved was his wrath. So red-hot, our devotion for God results in red-hot righteous and holy living as naturally as apple trees produce apples[15]. In that way our lives talk love before our lips do.

Matt Huesmann and Grant Cunningham[16] in their song, "Saving Grace," put it like this. "Faith requires selfless love for a world that's dying to see the hope in you in me." Meaning, people would believe God is real when they feel his touch of love through us. Only love, unconditional acceptance and care for people, shows people who Jesus is (see chapters 17-22 above)[17].

What's more, contagion isn't a monopoly of viruses. Sinners saved and transformed by grace could be winsome and contagious. Jesus was. We need prayer for that, don't we?

Why prayer?

Only in prayer can we know better and reflect better the God who prays unembarrassed. William Dunn Longstaff[18] in a hymn, "Take time to be holy" in "Hymns of Faith" had urged in stanza 2. "Take time to be holy, the world rushes on; Spend much time in secret with Jesus alone. By looking to Jesus like him you shall be; your friends, in your conduct, his likeness shall see." Take time.

Jesus, God, took early morning hours and sometimes whole nights to pray. Enthroned, he continues to pray. Apparently that isn't enough prayer. The Spirit, who is also God, joins Jesus, praying. Still that's not enough. The Scriptures demand that we must pray at all times Spirit-led. Then we would pray as God wants[19]. It appears the only one who doesn't pray is God the Father.

But he is the one who ordered Spirit-led prayer. "Call on me in the day of trouble; I will deliver you"[20]. God answers to strengthen, protect or rescue God's agenda—Jesus, the Spirit or Jesus' representatives (you and me); and self-imposed weakness and love—under attack in the conflict. God-defiance might resent it. But even they would admit this is legitimate, not arbitrary, use of supreme power.

That's why the God-defiant are delighted when we crowd out prayer, Christ-like desperate prayer for authentic survival[21] in our daily lives. For then we succumb powerless to enticements of our societal, political, and religious, God-defiance (see chapters 1, 11-15, 19 and 22).

But Psalm 50:15 says something else. "Call on me in the day of trouble," says God. "I will deliver you, and you shall glorify me." To be different, swim against the current in our daily associations (see chapters 17-22), puts us in trouble, conflict, daily. The promise of rescue anticipated that reality and another reality.

The other reality is a basketful of praises. Verse 23 said so. "He who brings thanksgiving as his sacrifice honors me." This is way over grocery lists and laundry baskets of prayer. It is celebrative joy and contentment, freedom and peace when ridiculed or ostracized for Jesus (see chapters 18, 19, 21, 22). That's how prayer as a way of life, praying and trusting and depending on God to do as he deems fit, gladdens God and us.

But supremely, lifestyle prayer completes our God-given lifestyle resistance, made up of the Spirit, self-imposed weakness, love and prayer, in the conflict. Like the other pieces, Spirit-led praying participates with God in what he's doing in the conflict. God is involved that's why we are. That shouts, where God (Jesus) and God (the Spirit) pray to God (the Father) is holy ground. But only the Spirit-led pull off their shoes and worship. Worship in awe, anticipating the day the Father totally and finally ends the conflict he had called.

Cited and Recommended References

Allen, Roland (1998). *Missionary Methods.* Grand Rapids: Wm B. Eerdmans.

Anderson, Neil (1990). *The bondage breaker.* Eugene: Harvest House Publishers.

Ankerberg, John and John Weldon (1993). *The Coming Darkness.* Eugene: Harvest House Publishers.

Awasu, Wilson (2003). *Fresh and Spicy.* Martinsville,: Airleaf Publishing.

Awasu, Wilson (1988). *Religion, Christianity and the Powers"* an nunpublished PhD Dissertation at Fuller Theological Seminary, Pasadena, California, USA

Berkhof, Hendrik 1962. *Christ and the Powers.* Scottdale: Herald

Brown, Rebecca (1987). *Prepare for War.* Chino: Chick Publishers.

Brown, Rebecca (1986). *He Came To Set The Captives Free.* Chino: Chick Publications

Buchanan, Mark (2001). *Your God is too Safe.* Sisters: Multnomah Publishers.

Caird, G.B. 1956. *Principalities and Powers.* Oxford: The Clarendon Press

Coggins, James R. and Paul Hiebert 1989. *Wonders and the Word.* Winnipeg: Kindred Press

Farrar, Stuart 1971. *What Witches Do.* New York: Coward, McCann and Georghegan, Inc

Frattarola, John 1987. "America's Best Kept Secret" in *Passport Magazine,* ed Derald Skinner

Fulbright, J. William 1966. *The Arrogance of Power.* New York: Vintage Books

Glasser, Arthur 1992. *Spiritual Conflict.* Downers Grove: InterVarsity Press

Hafstede, Geert (1997). *Culture and Organizations.* New York: McGraw-Hill.

Harper, Michael 1970. *Spiritual Warfare.* Plainfield: Logos International

Hesselgrave, David J. (1980). *Planting Churches Cross-Culturally.* Grand Rapids: Baker Books

Hiebert, Paul G. 1982. "The Flaw of the Excluded Middle" in *Missiology;* an International Review vol. X, No 1, January

Hiebert, Paul 1992. "Spiritual Warfare: Biblical Perspectives" in *Mission Focus,* Vol 20, No 3

Irvine, Doreen 1973. *From Witchcraft to Christ.* Cambridge: Concordia Press

Irvine, Doreen 1986. *Spiritual Warfare.* Basingstoke: Marshall Pickering

Jacobs, Cindy (1991). *Possessing the gates of the Enemy.* Grand Rapids: Chosen Books.

Johnson, Jerry 1989. *The Edge of Evil.* Dallas: Word Publishing

Kallas, James (1966). *The Satanward View.* Philadelphia: The Westminster Press.

Kallas, James (1968). *Jesus and the power of Satan.* Philadelphia: The Westminster Press.

Kallas, James (1975). *The real Satan.* Minneapolis: Augsburg Publications.

Kearney, Michael 1984. *WorldView.* Novato: Chandler & Sharp Publishers, Inc.

Kraft, Charles 1987. "Worldview and Spiritual Power" an unpublished paper at Fuller Theological Seminary, Pasadena, California, USA

Kraft, Charles 1989. *Christianity with Power.* Ann Arbor: Servant Publications

LaVey, Anton Szandor 1969. *The Satanic Bible.* New York: Avon Books

LaVey, Anton Szandor 1985 "Straight from the Witch's Mouth" in *Magic, Witchcraft and Religion* eds. Arthur C. Lehmann and James E. Myers. Palo Alto: Mayfield Publishing Company

Lausanne Committee 1985. "The Willowbank Report—Gospel and Culture" *Lausanne Occasional Papers No. 2,* Lausanne Committee for World Evangelization

Logan, Kevin 1988. *Paganism and the Occult.* Eastbourne: Kingsway Publications

Longstaff, William Dunn (1822-1894). "Take time to be holy" in *Hymns of Faith,* Scripture Union, 130 City Road, London, EC1V 2NJ

MacGregor, G.H.C. 1954. "Principalities and Powers: The Cosmic Background of Paul's Thought" NTS 1:17-28

MacNutt, Francis (1995). *Deliverance from Evil Spirits.* Grand Rapids: Chosen Books.

Medved, Michael 1992. *Hollywood VS America.* New York: HarperCollins Publishers, Inc.

Michaelsen, Joanna 1982. *The Beautiful Side Of Evil.* Eugene: Harvest House Publishers

Morrison, Clinton 1960. *The Powers that be: Earthly Rulers and Demonic Power in Romans 13:1-7.* Nashville: Harper and Brothers

Newbigin, Lesslie 1966. *Honest Religion for Secular Man.* Philadelphia: Westminster Press

Niebuhr, Reinhold (1960). *Moral Man and Immoral Society.* New York: Charles Scriber's Sons.

Penn-Lewis, Jessie 1973. *The Warfare with Satan.* Fort Washington: Christian Literature Crusade

Penn-Lewis, Jessie 1985. *War on the Saints.* Fort Washington: Christian Literature Crusade

Peretti, Frank (1986). *The Present Darkness.* Westchester: Crossway Books.

Phillips, Phil 1986. *Turmoil in the Toybox.* Lancaster: Starburst Publishers

Phillips, Phil 1991. *Saturday Morning Mind Control.* Nashville: Thomas Nelson Publishers

Piper, John, (1997). *A Godward Life.* Sisters: Multnomah Publishers

Piper, John (1993). *Let the Nations be Glad.* Grand Rapids: Baker Books.

Porter, David 1988. *User's guide to the Media.* Leicester: Inter-Varsity

Prior, David 1987. *Jesus and Power.* London: Hodder and Stoughton

Spieth, Jacob (1906). *Die-Ewe Stamme.* Berlin: Dietrich Reiner (Ernest Vohsen).

Spink, Kathryn (1997). *Mother Teresa.* San Francisco: HarperSanFrancisco.

Stewart, James 1951. "On a Neglected Emphasis in New Testament Theology" SJT: 292

Stott, John (1979). *The Message of Ephesians.* Leicester: Inter-Varsity Press.

Valiente, Doreen 1973. *The ABC of Witchcraft Past and Present.* Phoenix: Phoenix Publishing, Inc.

Wagner, C. Peter (1991). *Engaging the Enemy.* Ventura: Regal Books.

Wagner, Rich (2005). *The Gospel Unplugged.* Grand Rapids: Revell.

Walls, Andrew F. (1996). *The Missionary Movement in Christian History.* Edinburgh: T & T Clark.

Warnke, Mike 1972. *The Satan Seller.* Plainfield: Logos International

Warnke, Mike 1991. *Schemes of Satan.* Tulsa: Victory House, Inc.

Watson, David 1980. *Hidden Warfare.* Eastbourne: Kingsway Publications

White, John 1987. *The Fight.* Downers Grove: InterVarsity Press

White, John 1988. *When The Spirit Comes With Power.* Downers Grove: InterVarsity Press

Willard, Dallas (1998). *The Divine Conspiracy.* San Francisco: HarperSanFrancisco.

Wink, Walter (1986). *Unmasking the Powers.* Philadelphia: Fortress Press.

Wink, Walter (1984). *Naming the Powers.* Philadelphia: Fortress Press.

Yogananda, Paramahansa 1946. *Autobiography of a Yogi.* Los Angeles: Self-Realization Fellowship Pub.

Notes

Introduction
1 (Isaiah 7:14)
2 (Isaiah 9:6)
3 (Jeremiah 31:15, compare Matthew 2:1-23)
4 (Matthew 2:13-23)
5 (Matthew 16:13-23)
6 (John 13:26-27)
7 (Genesis 3:15)
8 (Isaiah 14:12-15)
9 (Isaiah 14:12-15)
10 (Revelation 2-3)
11 (John 20, Ephesians 1:19-23)
12 (Revelation 6:9-11)
13 (John 8:44)

Chapter 1
1 (see Walter Wink 1984, 1986)
2 (Galatians 6:1-2)
3 (1 Samuel 15:22-23)
4 (John 6:63)
5 (Matthew 15:1-9, 23:13-15)
6 (Isaiah 55:8-9)

Chapter 2
1 (Luke 4:18-19)
2 (Deuteronomy 13:1-11)
3 (Luke 4:28-30)
4 (John 7:53-8:2)

5 (John 8:3-57)
6 (John 8:58-59)
7 (John 10:31-39, compare John 11:45-53, 12:9-11, 12:57)
8 (Matthew 21:23-46)
9 (Matthew 22:15-46)
10 (Luke 22:1-6)
11 (John 18-19)
12 (Matthew 27:15-26, compare Mark 15:6-15, John 11:45-48, 12:10-11)
13 (Matthew 2)
14 (Exodus 32, 1447 BC; 1 Kings 12-22, 931 BC)
15 (2 Kings 21-25, 697-642 BC)
16 (2 Kings 17, 722 BC; 2 Kings 24-25, 586 BC)
17 (Genesis 11)
18 (Genesis 6-10)
19 (Genesis 4-5)
20 (Genesis 3)

Chapter 3
1 (Ephesians 1:20-21)
2 (Ephesians 3:10)
3 (Revelation 19:11-20:15)
4 (Genesis 1:28, compare Genesis 3)
5 (Revelation 1:18)
6 (Matthew 20:18, compare Luke 4:5-8)
7 (see John 5:19-24, Romans 8:33-34 and Revelation 20)
8 (Matthew 5:11-12)
9 (2 Timothy 3:12 compare 1 Peter 4:14)
10 (Genesis 4:1-16)

11 (Acts 7:51-60)
12 (Matthew 23:29-35)
13 (Revelation 6:9-11)
14 (See Arthur Glasser 1992)
15 (Ephesians 3:10)
16 (Mark 3:27, Colossians 1:13)
17 (2 Corinthians 4:4, 1 John 3:8)
18 (Ephesians 2:13-22)
19 (John 17:20-23)
20 (Revelation 21)
21 (Revelation 20:7-10 compare 12:9)
22 (1 Corinthians 2:8)
23 (Matthew 12:25-30)

Chapter 4
1 (Luke 22)
2 (Acts 5)
3 (Matthew 26:24)
4 (1 Samuel 28:3-25)
5 (see 1 Samuel 15:1-35)
6 (1 Samuel 16:14)
7 (Matthew 16:16-17)
8 (Matthew 16:21-23)
9 (Genesis 3)
10 (Matthew 12:22-37)
11 (John 8:44)

Chapter 5
1 (Mark 1:21-28, 5:1-20, 16:9, etc.)
2 (Matthew 10:1-42 and Luke 10:1-16)
3 (Luke 10:18-19)

4 (Acts 16:16-18)
5 (Acts 19:13-17)
6 (compare Jesus' insistence on the prerequisite of "prayer and fasting" in Matthew 17:14-21)
7 (Frank E. Peretti, 1986; C. Peter Wagner, 1991; John Ankerberg, & John Weldon, 1993; Cindy Jacobs, 1991)
8 (Francis MacNutt, 1995; Rebecca Brown, 1987; Neil Anderson, 1990)
9 (Charles Kraft, 1987; John Dawson, 1989)
10 (George Otis, 1999; Tom White, 1992; C. Peter Wagner, 1991)
11 (see Matthew 12:22-37)

Chapter 6
1 (Deuteronomy 18:10-12a)
2 (Acts 8:4-24)
3 (Acts 13:1-12)
4 (Acts 19:11-20)
5 (see the experience of the church in Thyatira, Revelation 2:19-29, and compare with Jeremiah 5:30-31)
6 (see Phillips 1986 and 1991 and Medved 1992)
7 (see Harper 1970)

Chapter 7
1 (the book of Job)
2 (Job 1)
3 (1 Samuel 16:14)
4 (Luke 13:10-17)
5 (2 Chronicles 18:1-34)

6 (1 Timothy 4:1)
7 (see Myth 3)
8 (Matthew 9:32-33)
9 (Matthew 12:22)
10 (Matthew 17:15)
11 (Luke 8:26-35)
12 (Mark 9:22)
13 (Mark 5:5)
14 (Mark 5:3-4 and Luke 8:39)
15 (Luke 13:11-17)
16 (John 8:28; Luke 9:39)
17 (Matthew 12:43-45)
18 (Luke 11:24-26)
19 (Mark 5:8, 11-13, Matthew 8:16, 28, and 33, Acts 8:6-7, and 16:16)
20 (Genesis 3:15, John 18-20)
21 (Matthew 8:29 compare Jude 6)
22 (Luke 10:17-20, compare with Acts 19:1-20)
23 (Acts 19:1-20)

Chapter 8
1 (Psalms 82:1 and 89:6, 8; Job 15:15, Deuteronomy 32:2 and Zechariah 14:5)
2 (Genesis 11)
3 (Genesis 12)
4 (Acts 17:24-26)
5 (verse 27)
6 (Romans 1:18-32)
7 (see Walter Wink 1984)
8 (Revelation 19:10, 22:8-9 compare Deuteronomy 6:4-9)

9 (Luke 12:11)
10 (Ephesians 1:21f, 2:1f, 3:10 and 6:12)
11 (Matthew 25:41)
12 (compare Matthew 12:22-29)
13 (Ephesians 2:1f)
14 (Romans 1)
15 (Deuteronomy 4:19)
16 (Deuteronomy 32:8)
17 (Daniel 10)
18 (compare Wink 1986)
19 (Green 1991:182)
20 (1979:274)
21 (compare Watson 1980)

Chapter 9
1 (Revelation 12:9, cf. John 12:31, 14:30 and 16:11, 1 Peter 5:8)
2 (2 Corinthians 4:4)
3 (1 John 5:19)
4 (Revelation 12:4, 9)
5 (Job 1:6-12 and Isaiah 14:12f)
6 (2 Corinthians 2:11, Ephesians 6:11, Revelation 2:24, compare James Kallas, 1966, 1968, and 1975; Walter Wink, 1984)
7 (Revelation 12:12 Matthew 4:6)
8 (see Job 1 and 2)
9 (compare Job 1:9-19, Isaiah 14:13-14, 1 Timothy 3:6, 2 Timothy 2:26, Revelation 12:7, 12 and 20:7)
10 (2 Thessalonians 2:9)
11 (1 Peter 5:8)
12 (2 Corinthians 11:14)

13 (Genesis 3)
14 (the book of Job)
15 (Jude 9)
16 (Zechariah 3)
17 (Matthew 4)
18 (Matthew 16:21-23)
19 (Luke 22:31f)
20 (Revelation 13, 17 and 20, cf. Daniel 7 and 2 Thessalonians 2, compare 1 John 4:3)
21 (1 Thessalonians 2:18)
22 (Acts 16:6)
23 (Leviticus 10)
24 (Joshua 7)

Chapter 10
1 (John 3:19-21)
2 (Genesis 3)
3 (Genesis 4)
4 (Genesis 6-10)
5 (Genesis 11)
6 (Genesis 3:15)
7 (the book of Exodus)
8 (the book of Esther)
9 (Matthew 2)
10 (Luke 4:1-13)
11 (Luke 22:1-6)
12 (John 18-19)
13 (Revelation 12:17)
14 (Acts 3-8)
15 (see the book of Jude)
16 (1 Timothy 2:1-7)

Chapter 11

1 (compare 1 Peter 2:13-14a)
2 (Revelation 20:7ff)
3 (Revelation 13:5-6)
4 (Revelation 13:2b)
5 (2 Thessalonians 2:9-10a)
6 (2 Thessalonians 2:7-10 and Revelation 13:5-8)
7 (Revelation 16:13-14)
8 (Ephesians 6:12)
9 (Matthew 24-25, Daniel 2 and 7, and Revelation 13:1-2, 17:7-17 and 20:1-6)
10 (Genesis 11)

Chapter 12

1 (Genesis 11)
2 (compare Wink 1984 and 1986)
3 (18th-20th centuries)
4 (1450-1873)
5 (1933-1945)
6 (1948-1994)
7 (see Wink 1986 and Fulbright 1966)
8 (1 John 2:18)
9 (1 John 4:3)
10 (2 Thessalonians 2:6-7)
11 (2 Thessalonians 2:6-7)
12 (1 Timothy 2:1-3)
13 (Romans 13)

Chapter 13

1 (1999)

2 (1992)
3 (1991)
4 (Francis MacNutt, 1995; Rebecca Brown, 1987; Neil Anderson, 1990)
5 (Charles Kraft, 1989; John Dawson, 1989)
6 (Frank E. Peretti, 1986; C. Peter Wagner, 1991; John Ankerberg, & John Weldon, 1993; Cindy Jacobs, 1991)
7 (compare Paul Hiebert 1992:45)
8 (Acts 11:1-3, compare Acts 10)
9 (Galatians 2:11f)
10 (Genesis 15)
11 (Genesis 16)

Chapter 14
1 (2 Thessalonians 2:3-10)
2 (1 Timothy 2:1-3)
3 (Romans 8:26-27, 34 and Hebrews 7:25)
4 (Acts 5:3, 9, 7:51, Ephesians 4:30, and 1 Thessalonians 5:19)
5 (Revelation 1-3)
6 (2:1-7)
7 (2:12-29)
8 (3:1-6)
9 (3:14-22)
10 (verses 3-19)
11 (2 Thessalonians 2:6-7)
12 (Isaiah 55:8-9, John 14-17, Romans 5-8, 12-13)
13 (2 Corinthians 4:4)
14 (John 3:16-24, Romans 13, Revelation 13)
15 (Matthew 23:1-7, John 5:44, 8:44 Romans 1:1-32)

16 (verses 20-21)
17 (verses 22-23)
18 (verses 24-25)
19 (Revelation 2:5, 16, 22, 3:3, 19)
20 (see Revelation 2:1-2, 8-9, 12-13, 18-19; 3:1-2, 7-8, 14-15; compare Isaiah 40, 53; Luke 2:33-35, Hebrews 4:12-13; and Revelation 1:12-16)
21 (compare Revelation 2:9-11, 3:8-13)
22 (compare Acts 8:4-26, 11:19-26, 13:1-12, and 1 Thessalonians 1:1-10)
23 (compare Jeremiah 2:4, 8, 11-13, 21)
24 (James 4:7-10)

Chapter 15
1 (Revelation 1-3)
2 (Ephesians 1:19-23)
3 (Isaiah 53:4-6, John 8:34-36, 14:6, Acts 4:12, 1 Timothy 2:5, 1 Peter 2:24)
4 (Luke 4:18-19, Ephesians 2:14-18, Colossians 1:15-20)
5 (John 17:20-23, 2 Corinthians 5:15 and 17, the book of Ephesians)
6 (Luke 23:36-53, Romans 1:16-17)
7 (Matthew 28:16-20, 1 Thessalonians 1:1-10, 2 Timothy 2:2)
8 (Colossians 1:13-14)
9 (Judges 16)
10 (2 Thessalonians 2:6-7, see above)
11 (Mark 12:29-31)
12 (John 13:34-35)
13 (Romans 12:9-21)

14 (1 Corinthians 13:4-8, Galatians 5:22-23, Ephesians 4)
15 (2 Peter 1:20-21, compare 2 Timothy 3:16-17)
16 (1975:65-108)

Chapter 16
1 (1972:362-371)
2 (2 Corinthians 11:14, compare wolves dressed like sheep, Matthew 7:15-20)
3 (Revelation 2:18-29)
4 (see Logan 1988, and Ankerberg and Weldon 1993)
5 (see 1 Samuel 29ff, 1 Kings 11ff and 2 Kings 21ff)
6 (Acts 13:1-3)
7 (Acts 8:4-24)
8 (Acts 19:1-20)
9 (Matthew 12:43-45)
10 (2 Corinthians 5:17)
11 (compare John 8:31-38)
12 (Titus 1:16)

Chapter 17
1 (Luke 4:1-13)
2 (Mark 1:23-25, 5:6-10)
3 (John 18-19)
4 (Matthew 12:46-50)
5 (John 7:1-9)
6 (John 4:1-42, 20:1-18)
7 (Luke 23:13-25, John 12:12-18)
8 (John 18-19)

Chapter 18
1 (Acts 4:19-20)
2 (Luke 24:36-53, Acts 1-4)
3 (Acts 1-8)
4 (Acts 9-15)
5 (Acts 11-28)
6 (LaTourette 1975:65-89)
7 (Acts 8)
8 (Acts 2, 10)
9 (Acts 13)
10 (Acts 17)
11 (Acts 14-18)
12 (see Dean Jones' "The Story of St. John," 1996)
13 (Matthew 5:11-12)
14 (2 Timothy 3:12)
15 (1 Peter 4:14)
16 (Revelation 6:10-11)

Chapter 19
1 (Mark 12:29-31, 1 John 4:20-21)
2 (John 17:20-23)
3 (John 4:1-42, Acts 1:1-8)

Chapter 20
1 (Isaiah 53:10-12, compare Luke 23:44-48, and Genesis 15:12, 17)
2 (Luke 23:33-39)
3 (Matthew 26:36-46)
4 (Matthew 27:45-46, John19:30)
5 (John 20, Ephesians 1:19-23)
6 (Luke 1:35)

7 (Luke 3:21-22)
8 (Luke 4:18-19, compare Isaiah 61:1-2)
9 (Zechariah 4:6)
10 (Matthew 12:22-32)
11 (John 5:19, 30)
12 (John 8:28-29)
13 (Luke 22:47-54 compare John 14:30-31)
14 (Luke 22-23)
15 (John 11:32-36)
16 (John 11:33)
17 (Mark 1:40-41)
18 (Luke 19:1-10)
19 (Luke 7:31-50)
20 (Matthew 23:37, Luke 19:41-44)
21 (Luke 23:34)
22 (John 15:13)
23 (John 13:34-35, compare 17:20-23)
24 (John 1:1-14)
25 (Matthew 26:39-46, John 14:30-31, compare the book of Isaiah)
26 (John 5:19 and 30)
27 (John 6:38)
28 (John 7:16-17)
29 (John 8:28-29)
30 (John 12:49-50, compare John 14:10, 30-31, 16:12-15)
31 (see the temptations, Matthew 4:1-11)
32 (Philippians 2:1-11)
33 (Hebrews 5:7-8)
34 (Matthew 14:23, Mark 1:35, Luke 6:12, 22:40-46, John 7:53-8:2, etc)

35 (Matthew 15:29-39, Mark 6:35-44, John 11:41-44)
36 (Luke 23:34)
37 (Luke 11:1)

Chapter 21
1 (Acts 1-2)
2 (see Acts 3-28)
3 (Acts 5)
4 (Acts 8:14-17)
5 (Acts 10:1-11:18)
6 (Acts 6:8-7:58)
7 (John 4:1-42)
8 (Acts 8:4-13)
9 (Acts 11:24)
10 (Acts 13:8-12)
11 (Acts 14:8-10)
12 (Acts 16:16-18)
13 (Acts 16:6-7)
14 (1 Thessalonians 2:8)
15 (Acts 5:32 compare Zechariah 4:6, Romans 15:18-19)
16 (John 3:25-30)
17 (John 12:10-11)
18 (Luke 19:8-10)
19 (Luke 18:28-30, compare Luke 5:1-11, 27-28, compare Matthew 5:16, Acts 4:13, 2 Corinthians 6:3-10, Philippians 3:7-11)
20 (Luke 8:2-3)
21 (Acts 16:13-15)
22 (Mark 14:3-9, compare Luke 7:37-38 and John 11:2)

23 (Acts 7:60)
24 (Acts 4:36-37)
25 (Acts 9:26-30, 11:25-26)
26 (Acts 15:36-39)
27 (Acts 8:4-5)
28 (Acts 11:19-21)
29 (Acts 13:1-3)
30 (Romans 9:1-3, 10:1-4, compare Exodus 32:30-32, Luke 19:41-44, 1 John 4:1-5:12)
31 (Acts 18:24-28)
32 (Romans 16:13-15)
33 (Acts 1:12-14, Acts 2:42, compare Luke 11:1-13)
34 (Acts 9:40)
35 (Acts 16:25-34)
36 (Ephesians 6:18-20)
37 (Jude 20-21)

Chapter 22
1 (Isaiah 55:8-9, John 14-17, Romans 5-8, 12-13, the book of Jude)
2 (see chapters 13-14, 16 above)
3 (see chapters 11-16 above)
4 (see chapters 7-10 above)
5 (see James 3:13-18)
6 (verses 20-21)
7 (verses 22-23)
8 (verses 24-25)
9 (Acts 6:8, 10)
10 (Matthew 20:28, compare 10:16 and 1 Corinthians 4:1-2, 2 Corinthians 4:1-12)
11 (John 4:7-5:5)

12 (Revelation 2:1-7)
13 (see the church in Corinth, 1 Corinthians 12-14)
14 (Acts 6:8 and 10, compare John 13:34-35, 17:20-23, 1 John 4:7-5:5)
15 (Acts 7:50)
16 (Acts 6:8-10)

Chapter 23
1 (see Genesis 3:15, Psalm 22, Isaiah 53)
2 (Genesis 3:15, Psalm 2, John 18-19, 1 Corinthians 2:8)
3 (see Philippians 2:1-11, compare with chapters 2, 17, 20 above)
4 (compare John Stott, 1979; and Wilson Awasu, 2003)
5 (Revelations 1:17-18)
6 (1 Corinthians 15, compare 1:18-2:16, and James Kallas, 1966, 1968 and 1975; Walter Wink, 1984)
7 (compare chapters 2, 17, 20 above)
8 (John 20, Ephesians 1:19-23)
9 (John 1 and Luke 1)
10 (John 3:1-21 compare John 4:1-42)
11 (Luke 24:36-53, Acts 1-2)
12 (see John 3:16, Romans 5:6-11, Colossians 3:12-14, David Prior, 1986; Mother Teresa in Spink, 1997)
13 (Luke 22:47-23:49)
14 (John 13:34-35)
15 (Luke 23:46)
16 (Ephesians 1:19-23)
17 (Romans 8:26-27, 34; Hebrews 7:25)

Chapter 24

1 (1 Peter 4:14, compare Matthew 5:10-12, Acts 5:40-41)
2 (John 4:24)
3 (John 17:3)
4 (Luke 24:36-43)
5 (Luke 24:44-45)
6 (Luke 24:46-47)
7 (Luke 24:48-49)
8 (Luke 24:50-53; see Awasu 2003:137-150 and Mark Buchanan 2001)
9 (Acts 7:51, Ephesians 4:30, 1 Thessalonians 5:19)
10 (Matthew 5:3)
11 (John 3:30 compare Luke 14:26, 27, 33; 2 Corinthians 12:9)
12 (see Matthew 10:16)
13 (2 Corinthians 4:5, 7)
14 (Mark 12:29-31 compare Luke 14:26, 27 and 33)
15 (John 14:21, 23, 17:3; 1 John 4:7-8, 11-12, 16, 19-21; compare Rich Wagner 2005)
16 (1998)
17 (compare Wagner 2005:220)
18 (1822-1894)
19 (Ephesians 6:18 compare Luke 18:1, John 15:16)
20 (Psalm 50:15 compare Luke 11:9-13)
21 (Hebrews 5:7-10 compare Romans 8:26-27)

Subject Index